RUBBER SIDE
DOWN

The Journey
(Photo by Michael Lichter)

RUBBER SIDE
DOWN

The Biker Poet Anthology

edited by
José (JoeGo) Gouveia

K. Peddlar Bridges – Submissions Editor
Susan Buck – Associate Editor

Archer Books
Los Angeles

Published in 2008 in the United States by
Archer Books
P. O. Box 1254
Santa Maria, CA 93456
www.archer-books.com – info@archer-books.com

Distributed in the United States by
Midpoint Trade Books, New York, NY
midpointbooksnyc.com

First Edition

Printed in the United States

Cover image: Michael Lichter

Cover design: JTC Imagineering

Library of Congress Cataloging-in-Publication Data

Rubber side down : the biker poet anthology / editors, José (JoeGo) Gouveia [and]
K. Peddlar Bridges. -- 1st ed.
    p. cm.
  ISBN 978-1-931122-19-1 (alk. paper)
  1. Motorcycling--Poetry. 2. Motorcycles--Poetry. I. Gouveia, José, 1964- II. Bridges,
K. Peddlar, 1947-

PN6110.M645R83 2008
808.81'008862928475--dc22

                                                                              2008024614

This anthology is dedicated to
Hunter S. Thompson and Allen Ginsberg
for their involvement with, and encouragement of,
the biker poetry movement.

Acknowledgments

All lines from ""First Party at Ken Kesey's with Hell's Angels" from *Collected Poems 1947-1980* by Allen Ginsberg. Copyright (©) 1965 by Allen Ginsberg. Reprinted by permission of HarperCollins Publishers.

"On the Move" from *Collected Poems* by Thom Gunn. Copyright © 1994 by Thom Gunn. Reprinted by permission of Farrar, Straus and Giroux, LLC.

Linda Lerner, "Critical Mass" from *Living in Dangerous Times* (Presa Press, 2007) by Linda Lerner. Copyright © 2007 by Linda Lerner. Reprinted by permission of the author.

Martin Jack Rosenblum, all poems by Martin Jack Rosenblum from *The Harley-Davidson Poems*, (Lion Publishing, 1989), licensed by Harley-Davidson. Reprinted by permission of the author.

Roger Vagnarelli, "Harley United" from *Leather, Wheels and Gravel-rash* (Arrival Press, UK, 1994) Copyright © 1994 by Roger Vagnarelli. Reprinted by permission of the author.

Diane Wakoski, "Uneasy Rider" and "The Desert Motorcyclist" from *The Motorcycle Betrayal Poems* (New York: Simon & Schuster, 1971). Copyright © 1971 by Diane Wakoski. Reprinted by permission of the author.

Many of the other poems and essays in this anthology have appeared previously in various periodicals and on a variety of Internet web sites. Copyrights for these and all other poems and essays in this collection reside with their respective authors. All have been reprinted herein by permission of those authors or their publishers.

Special Thanks from the Editor

First, to my parents, Joseph and Mary Gouveia, who have been there for me all along. They've always said to make something out of my life....here's the book! Marge Piercy & Ira Wood, for helping make this book possible. They have always been supportive in all my endeavors and I am fortunate to have them as friends. Martín Espada, another dear friend, who continually encouraged me to make this book happen at times when I was ready to give up. His words of support kept me going. Alicia Ostriker, my poetry 'godmother,' for her love and support over the years. She told me that my voice is important and encouraged me to write more "bad boy poems." Maxine Kumin, with whom I workshopped two biker poems. She supported my work, gave great feedback, and never judged me. Gerald Stern for his kindness, suggestions and conversations. His acceptance of a Biker Poet in academia meant much to me. Anne Waldman, for teaching me how to make poems work on the page and that not everything about poetry is performance. She pushed me to be a better writer, for which I am grateful. Diane DiPrima, for her kindness and pointing my attention to more biker poetry, particularly that of Freewheelin' Frank Reynolds, which broadened my horizons of biker poetry history. K. Peddlar Bridges, Submissions Editor of this anthology, who does so much for so many poets. His heart is always in the right place. Colorado T. Sky, for bringing me into the Highway Poets Motor Cycle Club and putting me on the road. He made a biker out of me. Susan Buck, Associate Editor, whose professionalism and keen eye in final editing and proofreading of this anthology made this a much better book. Martin Jack Rosenblum, who showered me with gifts of old posters of *The Harley-Davidson Poems*, two first editions of the book and his CD's. I treasure those gifts and encourage all to look up his poetry and music online. You'll be glad you did. And most importantly, to my daughter Alyssa, an awesome tattoo art-ist! She's inked my skin 4 times, each time inspiring a new poem. She is beautiful and talented, and I love her. And, of course, thanks to everyone who has published, booked, or written about the biker poets.

"The perfect man? A Poet on a Motorcycle."
—*Lucinda Williams*

"Faster, faster, faster, until the thrill of speed
overcomes the fear of death. . . ."
—*Hunter S. Thompson*

". . . to all those men who betrayed me at one time or another,
in hopes they will fall off their motorcycles and break their necks."
—Diane Wakoski, *The Motorcycle Betrayal Poems*

Table of Contents

Introduction

I first heard about the Highway Poets Motor Cycle Club (HPMCC) and its founder, Colorado T. Sky, in 1993 after a divorce in Florida brought me back to my home state, Massachusetts, and Cape Cod. With fewer responsibilities, I saw an opportunity to start life fresh and enrolled at Cape Cod Community College with the specific intent of furthering my poetic ambitions.

Once on campus, I was shocked to see very little happening in regard to poetry. My best friend, the now-deceased M. Scott Oickle, decided to start up a student-run poetry club that would later become the North Ground Poets, publishing student poetry anthology chapbooks. Scott and I spent many hours until sunrise working on our poetry, each other's works, and plotting our schemes for getting the student's words *out there*. In that process, many campus faculty and Cape Cod literati types kept mentioning this dude named "Sky" as someone I had to meet.

By the time 1996 rolled around, I was getting ready to graduate and transfer to UMass Dartmouth. Scott had been diagnosed with colon cancer.

In September '97, I started up a new poetry venue, with open mic, at The Prodigal Son Coffeehouse in Hyannis, MA. This establishment would become known as a mecca for poetry on Cape Cod, competing with another at the local community college. These two poetry scenes naturally melded together, as I had to build an audience at the Prodigal, and find poets to perform there, particularly in its inaugural year.

Rubber Side Down

Around the same time, I learned that the above mentioned "Sky" had enrolled full time at the college, and that he and some buddies had taken over the poetry club Scott and I had organized. I knew it was time for this alumn to revisit the campus, in search of one Colorado T. Sky.

I'll never forget that day. I spotted him immediately—clad in leather with biker patches, the long hair & beard, the eye patch, the tattoos, the brace on his leg and that loud raspy voice! I introduced myself, though he had already heard of me through campus faculty, and told him of my poetic vision. His response, "You sure you want me involved? I mean, I'm probably the most dysfunctional person you're ever gonna meet." That sealed the deal. I knew this guy was the real thing, and we have been close friends ever since.

As the poetry scene thrived, more poets came. The Summer of '97 found me hosting an International Poetry festival on Main St., Hyannis, in Richard's Galleries. At Sky's suggestion, co-founder of the Highway Poets and founder of RoadPoet E-magazine K. Peddlar Bridges was featured.

Peddlar is a quieter version of Sky, mellow, reserved (until he gets on stage) and always with an expression of deep thought in his eyes. We talked, mostly me answering his questions, as if I were in some sort of friendship interview. I passed, as he agreed to serve as an editor of this volume with me.

Both these guys kept telling me, "we need to get you some handlebars!" I had always wanted to ride, but the memory of my cousin losing his leg in a bike wreck when I was 12 kept me away. Finally, at age 39, I overcame that fear and—with everyone accusing me of going through a mid-life crisis—I bought my first bike. Now at 44, I've put tens of thousands of miles between 2 bikes (first a Suzuki GS750, now a Harley-Davidson Low Rider FXRS) and the desire to ride, write and perform is stronger than ever.

I've also befriended biker poets, like J. Barrett (Bear) Wolf who performed music at The Prodigal before revealing himself as a poet, he's always a crowd favorite. As I rode on, I met biker poets like Betsy (GypsyPashn) Lister in western Massachusetts, Marc (Moshe) Goldfinger in Boston, Susan Buck in New York, all of whom are treasured members of the Highway Poets MCC.

Introduction

I discovered the poetry and music of "The Holy Ranger" Martin Jack Rosenblum at Peddlar's direction. When we spoke on the phone for the first time he was pleasant, appreciative and humble —traits not expected in the stereotypical biker.

But that is, in fact, part of what this anthology is about. In these biker poets, I found diverse backgrounds and personalities. The movies of the 1960s and 1970s may have stereotyped the biker, but you'll ride a completely different road with us here!

I began compiling this anthology by e-mailing my network and posting to online forums. I never expected the messages to travel so far that this book would represent biker poets from Australia, China, Holland, England, Belarus, South Africa, three provinces of Canada and every corner of the United States.

For example, Nikolai Ivanovich "Nikita" Karpukovich is retired from the Russian army, having served as an M.D. at the Chernobyl disaster site. Cecil "Speedo" Plaatjies was imprisoned on Robben Island with Nelson Mandela and Dennis Brutus for fighting apartheid. Ian MacIan is the HPMCC National Secretary of Australia & New Zealand where he is a journalist for Christian publications, and has won awards for scientific writing. Wu "Woo Wu" Hai Tien is a former Chinese Bureau Chief and one of the first reporters covering the 2004 India Ocean Sumatra Tsunami. All the others have equally distinct backgrounds, but enjoy enjoy two things in common: they all ride motorcycles and write poetry.

All in all, over 300 pages of biker poetry were submitted from across the globe, from which the poems herein were selected. Some of the poets are well known, while others are not. But this anthology is not meant to be definitive. Many biker poets are missing. The legendary, late great Freewheelin' Frank Reynolds, Hunter S. Thompson (to whom this book is dedicated, along with Allen Ginsberg) and Michael McClure are but a few who come to mind.

Biker poets have probably existed in the archetype of the troubadour since the motorcycle was invented. But it wasn't until Sky and Peddlar formed the HPMCC with a vision of unifying and promoting it as a movement that biker poetry rode into the culture's consciousness. In the 1980's, Peddlar dragged biker poets on stages and Sky published them in the Highway Poet magazine. Peddlar to this day continues publishing many of us online and in biker magazines, Sky has published two other books and several CDs of his work.

MarySusan Williams-Migneault at RdHousePress.com has been publishing and promoting biker poetry since 1986, and Wild Bill Rogers in Alaska includes biker poets in every publication he works on. And, there are many others, too numerous to mention. This anthology is my humble contribution to a growing tradition of writing, riding, publishing and working the life of a biker poet.

Finally, since this book is already in your hands, you get it and, if you don't already have your own, you may be next in line for "getting some handlebars."

Enjoy the ride!

—JoeGo

Foreword

Outsider Poetics:
Motorcycle Voices Sound This Way

Rubber Side Down is a good title.

It is an expression between motorcyclists that means *ride safely* and signifies that, as in *keep the rubber side down*, we shall meet again at the next café for coffee or swap meet for spare parts—if we have kept it down safely. Or have stayed upright, as it were, as we move on tires toward the same sort of horizon that cowboys in the old West (romanticized or not) headed for to evade civilization (never romanticized).

It once was a merciful, secret salutation and by now has been colonized mercilessly. But somehow the writers in this collection manage to witness experience on a motorcycle not only from the saddle, but once the ride is done by daybreak or begun as night falls on roads going everyplace but home.

The idea is that home is a place with spatial memories and that the road remembers nothing but having been upon it. The more one rides, the less being confined is worth the remembrance. Cars are 'cages.' One does not ride an automobile; riding in an auto is the way it goes. It is another homey space. There always has been something about The Outsider in every motorcyclist, no matter if it is Gene Vincent within Rockabilly, setting the stage for black leather jacketed music with a busted leg from a motorcycle that did not keep its rubber side down, or Bob Dylan escaping the world of Blonde On Blonde gone mad—a Post-Modernist crash away from popularity into a period of tapes in the basement that created Rock music all over again when the rubber left the bottom side and toppled, permitting escape and better wandering.

Rubber Side Down

The poetry in this book is written by folks who are outside the cultural safety zones. Some ignore technique, some deplore it; some explore it beyond where workshop academics would confine it and some take a breather from the understood confines of a literary canon sensibility to gather a better voice because of a crazy, two-wheeled power drift into experiential reverie.

Motorcycles are not supposed to stay balanced unless there is movement. That's physics. Motorcycles are perhaps objects d'art to some who have not fallen over just yet, but to those who have and get back on and go they are epiphanies with horsepower. That's metaphysics. If you are wrongly educated, you will find folk art of some kind in these pages. If you are not, you will find familiarity if you are a rider, and honesty if you are not.

There are great poets who ride motorcycles and some are in this book. And there are great motorcyclists who are not poets at all, because they have chosen to be as silent as where the next road takes them, leaving it all behind in wonder. Yet, as William Carlos Williams once put it, silence is complex but you do not get far with silence.

These poets in this book go far and have kept poetry loud and original through the decades, even if the bikes themselves have been severely marketed, put into art galleries upon pedestals and within museums behind glass, and inside sociology books that have weak spines because they are too thick. Motorcycle poets have voices that sound this way. As authentic Outsiders, their poetics resemble gravel caught in a belt drive. Or back when, in a chain. Then or now, something is about to throw you. So keep the rubber side down.

This book is a swap meet. What do you have in trade for parts of its knowledge?

—Martin Jack Rosenblum

RUBBER SIDE
DOWN

On The Move 'Man, You Gotta Go.'

Thom Gunn

The blue jay scuffling in the bushes follows
Some hidden purpose, and the gush of birds
That spurts across the field, the wheeling swallows,
Have nested in the trees and undergrowth.
Seeking their instinct, or their pose, or both,
One moves with an uncertain violence
Under the dust thrown by a baffled sense
Or the dull thunder of approximate words.

On motorcycles, up the road, they come:
Small, black, as flies hanging in heat, the Boy,
Until the distance throws them forth, their hum
Bulges to thunder held by calf and thigh.
In goggles, donned impersonality,
In gleaming jackets trophied with the dust,
They strap in doubt—by hiding it, robust—
And almost hear a meaning in their noise.

Exact conclusion of their hardiness
Has no shape yet, but from known whereabouts
They ride, directions where the tires press.
They scare a flight of birds across the field:
Much that is natural, to the will must yield.
Men manufacture both machine and soul,
And use what they imperfectly control
To dare a future from the taken routes.

It is part solution, after all.
One is not necessarily discord
On Earth; or damned because, half animal,
One lacks direct instinct, because one wakes
Afloat on movement that divides and breaks.
One joins the movement in a valueless world,
Crossing it, till, both hurler and the hurled,
One moves as well, always toward, toward

A minute holds them, who have come to go:
The self-denied, astride the created will.
They burst away; the towns they travel through
Are home for neither birds nor holiness,
For birds and saints complete their purposes.
At worse, one is in motion; and at best,
Reaching no absolute, in which to rest,
One is always nearer by not keeping still.

Heavy Lean
Daniel A. Armstrong

I remember the summer of '78
    That was the year
    Van Gogh lost his ear
See he and Gaugin both had it
    Bad for the same girl,
    Betty Lou Beaujolais—
She was from an old wine family
    And moonlighted as a
    Bare-blue-footed can-can dancer
    On starry, starry nights
    At the Beachcomber Bistro & Burlesque
    but I digress. . . .
Anyway, Vinny and G. both had it bad for her
    Right?
So they decided to race to determine
    Who'd ask her out.
Up in the hills above Monaco they met on their
    Da Vinca 750's
    The chamomile exhaust sweet in the mid summer's air
A purloined piece of the Shroud of Turin
    Was the starting flag—held by
    A little Italian boy who would grow up to invent
    The wireless so that just such contests
    Could one day be broadcast to hundreds
    Maybe thousands of people
Un!
Deux!
Trois!
Aaaaaaaaaaaaaaaaaaaaand they're off!!!
With a sound like bog-born bullfrogs
    G. in an early, two length lead
    Vinny, low behind the fairing
    Ducking G.'s dusty tail

Fast and clean, he's in a heavy lean
He's in a heavy lean

In & out of turns their flight
    A race started early, lasting all night
    'til the last hard turn in
    this match bizarre
    that would one day shoot
    Grace Kelly's star
They're in a heavy lean, they're in a heavy lean

But G. couldn't hang the turn so close
And what happened next, do you suppose?
G.'s bike righted, taking roadless flight
While Vinny held on with all of his might
Leanin' so heavy, the road so near -
Vinny made the turn, but he lost his ear

He's in a heavy lean, a heavy lean

Then quick he was, across the line
Through cheers, confetti and serpentine!

Well, that Italian kid, he grabbed the ear
And delivered it fast to the maiden dear
Who held it to Vinny's head, from whence the road peeled it
Then kissed it and held him and by her love healed it.

Now I know that you're all concerned about G.
But he's okay, spent the night in a tree
Waiting for the folks from town
While they built a scaffold to bring him back down

And so in marriage ends our story, and not in woe
The hyphenated nuptials of Vincent, and
    Betty Lou Beaujolais-Van Gogh!

Sidecar Riding

Paula Doherty

sailing through space
in the seat of the sidecar
I smell the hot engine &
growling exhaust—
I tip back my head
& watch The Big Dipper
pouring night's beauty
all over our ride.

Smelling of Sweet Grapes and Wildness

Paula Doherty

I spied
on my little ride—
farmstand gladioli
reaching

grey heron's solemn stillness
sunset's
saltmarsh shadows.

stone walls in ordered collapse
Heaven's ribbon-twisting
between raggedyshorn cornfields

darkening sky mysteries
smelling
of sweet grapes & wildness.

The Battered Pylon

Denis J. Dunn

a gorgeous fall day of motorcycling—
gliding slickly through the highway maze
of orange & black pylons—
i'm starting to think,

"i'm getting the hang of this!"
     whoooosh, to the left
     whoooosh, to the right
all without hitting a single sweaty hard hat—

so here i am slaloming & sashaying along
when suddenly i come upon
a woman sitting cross-legged lotus position
by the side of the road
replete with orange vest & red octagon stop sign
perched atop a tall yellow pole—

so transfixed was i by this interspersion
of the eternal into the everyday
that i lost my zenlike manipulation of handlebar
and ran over & crushed the last pylon in line,

turning its noble jutting nose
into an awkward accordion.
rear-viewing, i backward glanced
expecting blue lights of retribution—
but what i saw was the orange cone
valiantly struggling to regain its dignity
like the face of a thumb-pressed baby doll
popping back from toddler distress.

throughout all of this buddha lady sat as calm & unperturbed as ever,
as a workman came & compassionately set the cone aright
awaiting the next opportunity to enlight.

Ride the Wind

Beth Groundwater

I hug the rumbling bike,
Open the throttle wide.
Howling wind whips leather
Against tense arms and thighs.
I lean into the turns.
White road stripes whoosh by.
The wheels leave the pavement,
Showing below, blue sky.
Ride, baby, ride.
No, fly, baby, fly.

A hawk swoops overhead.
Challenging me, it cries.
"Come soar and hunt with me,
Search for where treasure lies."
From my twitching shoulders
Massive black wings unfurl.
They whip a magic beat.
I soar, take flight and whirl.
Ride, baby, ride.
No, fly, baby, fly.

We suck in the same air,
That screaming hawk and I.
Wind roars across my ears.
Swelled with freedom, I sigh.
I scan the ground below.
Tall pines sway, knock and creak.
A fox flushes a mouse.
The hawk dives, steals the treat.
Ride, baby, ride.
No, fly, baby, fly.

Too soon, I sink back down,
Engine between my thighs.
The hawk, in tribute, dips
Feathered sails in the sky.
Did it really happen?
 "Who cares!" I shout with verve.
I throw my head back, laugh,
and roll around a curve.
Ride, baby, ride.
No, fly, baby, fly.

Critical Mass

Linda Lerner

a guy jumped on a bike in San Francisco
didn't know where / why
a few hundred others came:
it was the last decade of the century
they begin wearing down
what asphalts the road. . . .

two days later, September 27th
my birthday in a candle-lit bedroom
I'm riding out a love story with a man
I'll be riding it out on paper
after he's gone
riding it back & forth
     everywhichway
to keep a heart beating. . . .

       across America
from Union Square North to
Washington Thompkins Madison Square parks
     cities across Europe
a few thousand cyclists began
riding out the century
thru the dead waste of
work day lives
auto politic exhaust fumes
what poisons the mind-breath

the last Friday of the month clear
the road that spans thru this country
our lives is our life line. . . .

I heard them as I sat in a Village cafe
looked out and saw
blazing metallic urban angels

clicking gears honking
down streets they emptied of cars trucks
flew without leaving the ground. . . .

never been on a bike like that
but know the sheer joy of
speeding down a road that doesn't exist
till I'm on it

is that what they feared
when cops hauled in 50 cyclists
before the republican convention
everyone tries to silence:

the roar of freedom
a road being cleared?

Harley United

Roger Vagnarelli

Not to them
Do tortured tones
Of twisted two stroke
Twins appeal;
Racer's crouch
Grand prix attire
Bright plastic
Wheel to wheel.

Who can deny
The virtues
Of obsession
In a marque,
Symbolic of
The freedom
Sought by those
In dark glasses.

Seated low
In upright posture,
Arms held high,
Feet to the fore,
Proud to live
Astride a legend
Rooted deep
In biker lore.

And in common
With like riders,
Who in the aura
Have delighted,
They remain an
Elite brotherhood,
Alike,
Harley united.

The Nomad

Wordwulf

See, they ride the steel wheel dragons
to the final rendezvous
The tears freeze to their faces,
they go ridin' two by two.
Captains take the black car,
then all the brothers come
The last steel dragon rider,
he come ridin' one by one
But he come ridin'

Through the iron gates of madness
as the Nomad comes to be
He cries, "By God, I'll find the man,
his blood will set you free!"
Sends the digger on his way,
"We bury our own, old son"
His hands will bleed the winter,
he come ridin' one by one
But he come ridin'

You can't replace a brother,
can't even say goodbye,
When someone's steel destroys him,
their cannon makes him die
He becomes the stuff of stories
as all his brothers mourn
And a lone steel dragon rider
rides into the storm
But he come ridin'

To be a part yet set apart,
the Nomad stands alone
He rides across the country,
his Harley is his home

When a brother needs a helping hand
he'll ride straight into the gun
Because he is a Nomad,
he comes ridin' one by one
but he come ridin'

Weather & Other Maps

J. Barrett (Bear) Wolf

I get in one last, quick ride
Before the hinting tumult of clouds coalesce
Into the thunder light show and falling
Bucket cat dog pianos of rain.

I urge past impending corn fields, earth brown
Recently tilled turning to face sun and receive the seed
Or green with grasses and yellow flowers
Like the thirteen and a half millionth dandelion
I passed on the way to Windsor.

Consider the asphalt tongue of the future.
It grins and swallows me into the miles and the days
Inches unremembered, though towns and times and faces
Never to be forgotten
Except the ones I did, until somebody says
"Ya remember when we. . . ?" And mostly I do.

Shadows disappear as the furl of overcast advances.

We are always paradox
Holding conflicting thoughts
Making choices as if we could know where they lead
There is no map quest for a way to live
No locator beacon in case of emergency
No chip in the industrial hominid cell phone
That will sort out the correct direction
Away from the storm.
Away from the dark.
Toward the love and home and picket damn fence
Someone to come in from the road to,
When we are caught off guard
And take that thunder lightning hit.

There is only so much we can predict.
Bet a trip into town on the weather map

Take the bike because the thrum of exhaust
And the thrum of rain will not intersect today.

But that is the trouble with weather, isn't it?
Knowing it is going to rain.
This time.

Tattoo Archeology

J. Barrett (Bear) Wolf

Miles, wires, the clicks of keyboard
Muses, myth, rumor and legend
Artifacts and ancestors lives,
loves and losses painted on body canvas
from Papua New Guinea to Newark New Jersey.

When we speak in skin verse we are of one voice
One—yet many hearts   knowing
places not so much secret, but avoided
by those content to leave no trace.

We strip off our mundane days
Bare ourselves as we receive the ink
Naked, lovingly, knowingly genuflecting
beneath honesty's bright blade,
slaking our appetite for painful truth.

Our histories are aboriginal marks, slash lines,
tribal glyphs and disney cartoons left on skin
to be seen but by others of the mark,
those few willing to go . . . deeper.

Some day they will read from our weathered hides
accounts of aching openness and infinite compassion
They will speak of distance between us with a lingering smile,
of howling loneliness the way we refer to plague,
some long forgotten malady . . .
referred to in ancient text.
Stories we could not tell in mere language
or leave to the predilections of perjurers
who would cast aspersions, like cheap spells, on our character
vexed as we redefine civilization as a skin condition.

We will be long gone then, to history, to legend.

Teachers for those whose yearning stretches
to caress our kindred spirits
to read the testament of our mirrored hearts
And we will be remembered...
Even when the tides are still and seasons change no more.

Evel Knievel

José "JoeGo" Gouveia

You stared death down
Over drag bars and cars,
10, 15, 20 at a time—
Launched greatness
From ramps of ambition,
Grit and mettle.
Breaking records
And 40 bones,
You denied death
For better job opportunities.

When the night officer,
Trying his hand
At poetry, nicknamed
You "Evil," because
It rhymed with "Knievel,"
Had he a clue the couplet
Would race down the gauntlet,
A former bank robber
Stealing fame to that name?

You stole the show
At Caesar's Palace,
Leaping the fountains
Of your youth,
Taking to the air
Rubber side down,
Shiny side up.
The landing threw
Our American Daredevil,
Clad in leather armor
Of red, white and blue,
From the sparkle of chrome
Forever into the Wild World of Sports.

Twenty-nine days comatose
Couldn't alter your ego—
The surgical steel
And fused backbone
Refused to bend.
With a will stronger
Than your welded frame,
You fed wonder
By the forkfuls
To young boys dreaming
Of being Evel.

Of course there was only one
Knievel, Man of steel and scars,
Superhuman and super-hero,
Not even the kryptonite
Of Snake River Canyon
Could dull your shine.
You twisted the throttle
Over death's domain,
Rose from the ruins
And river the Ferryman
Dared not cross, not even
Your look was defeated.

The crashes could not kill,
Hepatitis could not kill,
Hard liquor
And harder women
Could not kill.
Lung disease
Could not kill.
You killed time
As time killed you,

Stalking your clock
Like a determined lover.

You said you found God,
"all of a sudden."
Thought of Him daily,
Forged your frail body
To a kneeling.
In youth jumping rattle-
Snakes and lions,
Fountains, cars and canyons—
At 69, taking practice runs
At a leap of faith.

If Peter denies you passage,
If your name
Doesn't appear
In the Guinness Book
Of Celestial Records,
We'll all look on
In awe from our
Meditative states,
Anticipating one last
Leap, over God's Gate.
And if your soul crashes
Into His throne,

In a shooting star
Of painless bliss,
A meteor shower
Of cosmic chrome
And lighting will forever
Highlight that long last leap
Into legend,

Leaving skidmarks
On the streets of gold,
And even God
Will cheer your name,

"Evel. . . ."

Baiku

José "JoeGo" Gouveia

> *Baiku: n.* A Biker lyric verse form having three unrhymed
> lines of five, seven, and five syllables, traditionally invok-
> ing an aspect of riding or biker life, or referring in some
> way to the nature of riding or riding season.

Jesus she's dirty!
bugs & mud splatter my bike-
Ah, riding season!

Laconia run
to the strip to see the show
bikes and boobs abound!

steel rubber and chrome
roaring through concrete jungles
thunder storms roll in

Harley-Davidson
Low Rider is where I found
God, a biker, man!

Loud and Proud straightpipes
Illegal the police say
I don't hear a word

Special construction
Forks raked out 6-inch over
Ape hangers keep cool

Joys of a Harley
The road the wrench the ride, man,
Don't settle for less

Shirt and tie man rides
He don't need no wrench at all
Just a riceburner

Kick stand up turn key
press starter button—no go?
Hey! Turn the gas on dummy!

The Silence of Straight Pipes

José "JoeGo" Gouveia

The sudden silence of straight pipes
And big twin 1340 cc's find us
Coasting into Craigville Beach
Her chin rises off my shoulder
Her hands clench fistfuls of Tee shirt
Spreads her legs out for balance
Uncertain where our weight will sway us

My right foot swings from highway peg
To rear brake pedal, my hand, like hers,
Squeezing, chrome to chrome front brake
Lever as she drops her foot we lean left stopping
She lifts herself asking "What's the matter?"

Pride proclaims, "It's an easy fix"
As I wiggle the wires from coil to
Spark plug, turn the key, tap on the
Carb, turn the key, twist the throttle,
Turn the key, check cable clutch,
"Routine check babe, don't worry"

"Could it be the battery?"
(Could it be? Could it be?)
"I just checked that" as I see
A pack of five bikers, two
I know, at the far end of the lot,
Laughing at me. "Do you know those guys?"
"No," because when a babe rides bitch
You don't ask for help you do it yourself
"You sure it's not the battery"

"The battery's new, don't worry,
It's an easy fix," but I'm clueless
And toolless and especially powerless
"All power has a source," with wisdom
I proclaim unclip the seat expose

The battery and a loose corroded wire

"I knew it wasn't the battery," I state
And she stares, "How do you fix that?
The wires has to go back on?"
I assure her it's under control

As I strip that wire with my teeth
Nervously she giggles and grins
"How you going to keep the wire there?"
I play like I don't know her
Wink as I ask her for her number
And if I can call her sometime
She hands me her business card
Which I roll like a joint twist and

Fold over twice and again crafting
A clip to wedge between terminal
And frame, holding that positive
Power line to its source- the lights go on
"You were right, it wasn't the battery"

I clip the seat in place
We strap our helmets on
I turn on the gas
We get on the bike
I turn the key
Kick the starter
Rev the throttle
As my straight pipes roar
Parked bikers swallow my sandstorm
Here at Craigville Beach
As I shout to her,

"Babe, this is how we get home."

Like Th' Bird 'E Sez About Philbert, His Scarlet Macaw

Ian MacIan, Secretary, HPMCC Chapter, Christchurch, NZ,

'S like I sez, just like, an' why'm say'n ¯at's¯
cuzzy assed, iz why. An' me, I sez,
I'll tellyez right enough!

An' so I did
    It's birds, an' 'ey're bloody sharp about it, too.
    Got li'l pinny brains, 'ey ave,
    Sma', they a', but p'inty, too.
    Is' quab I 'ad, f' years an' years,
    'an 'ated me, each an' ev', 'struth.
    'uz ever time I'd see'm 'ere,
    I'd whistle a shrilly two-tone third
    just in the way of an "owdya do?"
An' later, once, whilst sudsin' at my local
    Another fancier I chanced to meet
    'oo tol' me 'bout the lingo o' the buzzards
    an' 'ow the feth'ry buggers tend t' speak
    this shrilly, trillin' t'ird wot I been whistlin'
    is a long and coloured curse in "Birdanese"
    so 'e teaches me a newer an' polite way
    more astute, polite, and guaranteed t' please
Well, this ol' long story's so enticing
    I'm implored to tell it time an' time again
    It always fascinates the li'l spuds at 'ome
    To think that I can speak in "Birdanese"
    An' stops 'em spellbound at the pub; where
    Albert asks me to smarten up 'is geese
    And at the summer tucker-up I'm always
    Asked about their humor and philosophies
A letter came by post one summer evenin'
    From some flattop in a flowing sort of robe
    'is letter sez 's an ornitho-linguist
    Whose been busy learnin' poesy from the birds
    And I fills 'im in on the little that I knows

An' 'e huffs at me an' looks way down
His long an' pimply nose an' sez, "see here,
It's just not possible that birds would talk to one like you."
So in a fluff of musty, dusty robes and a dangle of his tassel
'pon 'is 'igh an' mighty ornitholo-jest
'e climbed, and from the mount of knowledge spew'd
that bird an' I wuz soundly fulla shite
an' 'e disappears back to the university
an' I, with shouldered my squab, in harmony
whistle him a shrilly, trilling two-tone third
to speed him on his merry musty way.

On Yon Quill Road

Nikolai "Nikita" Karpukovich,
HPMCC Member-at-Large, Minsk, Belarus

"Why I am a Highway Poet," written at Johns Garage

Not an easy path, God knows.
    Voraciously insatiable,
Quill Road selects
    its travelers, victims
destined for the mystic cryptic paths,
    paved in pain, in ink, in blood, in gasoline.
The load the weight
    of time times humanity
borne on the brains
    of those vagabond poets
with their lives on the lines
    that mark the lanes and their passage
down through the cosmic
on Yon Quill Road.

The Six-Legged Moose
Wild Bill Rogers

The wildlife in Alaska is something to behold.
Of those critters in the north stories have been told
Of interactions 'tween the fauna and two legged folks.
I've got a story for ya' I've been promised ain't' no hoax.

A certain scooter tramp with a stubborn reputation
Was on his first spring ride after winter's hibernation.
He left his place in Anchorage riding the Old Glenn
Headin' north to Palmer to get out in the wind.

No rain fell on that day it was really warm and clear
So he pulled her in at Klondike's and had himself a beer.
If you've been to Klondike's you know one ain't' enough
So that part of the story one might wish to rebuff.

After leaving Palmer he stopped in Sutton Town
And has some more refreshments to wash the others down.
The spring celebration left his mind a little foggy.
I heard his condition described as somewhat soggy.

He got up past King River towards the Chickaloon
When he came upon a critter in a place inopportune.
A moose stepped in the road at that bikers ETA
Staring straight at his Harley with clear intent to stay.

Bullheaded by their nature they're an ornery lot.
But that biker, he was oiled, pigheaded and hot!
The biker called that moose every name in the book.
The moose just stood there staring with a defiant blank look.

When obvious to the biker the moose would never budge
He made a rash decision; he would give that moose a nudge.
Rapping up his pipes to scare the moose with sound
He took off burning rubber, just as that moose turned round.

When moose and bike are north bound and their destinies inter-
twined
It paints an ugly picture when painted from behind
The bike stop's kinda' sudden the biker starts to sail
And headfirst hits that moose just beneath the tail.

Now bear in mind it ain't' my yarn it's probly' just a fable.
One of those critter stories that's told around the table.
But in that story I suspect you will find the roots
Of the Six Legged Moose wearing motorcycle boots.

Michael Lichter
Photo Section

Michael Lichter (www.lichterphoto.com) began photographing custom bikes and the biker lifestyle after merging passions for photography and Harleys in 1977. In the years since, *Easyriders* magazine has printed over 800 articles with his work, he has done calendars, illustrated eight coffee table books, provided images to countless companies in the industry and may now be the most published photographer of this genre in the world. In 2001, Michael began exhibiting limited edition lifestyle prints in galleries across America and abroad.

FACES, CITY PARK, STURGIS, SD., 1980

City Park was a world of its own and a protective sanctuary for many. Once inside its gates, very little existed beyond. Such an odd collection of personalities, backgrounds, and faces. Was this the heart of America in 1980?

EARLY MORNING, CITY PARK, STURGIS, SD. 1979

I arrived in Sturgis for my first bike week too late to see the lay of the land but just in time for the all night party that happened every night in City Park. This then was my first morning in Sturgis. I woke up not having slept much and assessed the damages, both internally and externally. What sort of toll did the party take? There was drag racing down the narrow pavement between the tents, there were campfires, wildness until all hours of the morning and a dreamlike recollection of police cars with lights flashing, screaming through the park in the middle of the night.

BOBBER AT THE BAR & LOUNGE, STURGIS, SD. 1979

With its powerful direct flash, I'm reminded of old newspaper and police evidence photographs. It could have been taken in 1947 during the Hollister incident, but this was still how Sturgis looked in 1979. I feel too young to have taken it.

HIGH BARS AT THE OASIS, STURGIS, SD. 1987

Magoo is a character that has always lived the life. "World Famous," his gas tank stated as he traveled the country tattooing in the 1980s. Two little dogs went everywhere with him tucked into his vest pocket. Twenty-five years have passed and he is still tattooing, only now, when his wife is busy sewing leather and it's his turn to care for the kids, two bulldogs help pull them around in a cart. And two dogs are still tucked in his pocket.

HARLEY BACK PIECE, HUMBOLDT, IA. 1999

Harley riders have a loyalty and pride of ownership that has brand managers at other companies green with envy. It is unique. The Harley logo is tattooed on arms, backs, tops of heads, and sensitive areas that don't see the light of day. It is displayed like a badge of honor and seen as an exclusive club membership.

SPORTSTER JOHN & ARLENE'S WEDDING, EVERGREEN, CO., 1980

When Sportster John and Arlene were married in Eldorado Springs, CO., the big question was would he still be "Sportster John" even though his bride surprised him with keys to a brand new Wide Glide. As part of the festivities we rode to the Little Bear in Evergreen but clouds moved in and we moved out. The moniker lasted. The marriage didn't.

CHOPPERS AT JUNCTION AND MAIN, STURGIS, SD, 1979

Where is everybody? Is this really the busiest corner in Sturgis on Saturday, the biggest day of the rally? Rossini went on to create his famous tattoo parlor in this barbershop and this corner went on to be the best corner for citizens, bikers and the police to watch the scene. Rossini passed away in 2003 and you don't see Honda choppers looking like this anymore, but the long front ends, metal flake, and pull back bars are back. If we wait long enough, any style is bound to return.

EVERYBODY'S TALKING, STURGIS, SD. 1991

The Ballad of California Slim and Nightstick Jim

J.H." Colorado T." Sky

Sit right there, bro
let me get you a brew
I heard a story
of interest to you

Now, I know you've been here
and you've been over there,
but gimme a listen
I'm cluin' ya square

Downeast in Maine
where the winters are grim
lives a righteous old biker
named California Slim

Ol' Slim, he's nasty
and covered with scars
that picked up in Asia
and various bars

But Ol' Slim, he's mellow
and he don't get loud
he tokes and he tanks
and he putts tall and proud

Now up in Slim's neighborhood
workin' the 'Pike
is a Highway Patrolman
that nobody likes

He's big and he's mean
but not like you and me
about five hundred pounds
and seven-foot three

and the folks 'round New England
all know about him
how he's fast with the club
and he's called Nightstick Jim

We all know how it is
between bikers and cops
harassment, entrapment
the shit never stops
and all the folks
for miles around
knew something heavy
would soon go down

Between the biker dude
named California Slim
and the monster cop
called Nightstick Jim

Now, I can tell a lot
by just lookin' at things
but the opera ain't over
'til the fat lady sings

It happened one morning
'bout quarter past three
while Slim was out puttin'
just catchin' some breeze

He'd had him a toke
and his head felt just right
alone on the road
in the yellow moonlight

his Pan singin' happy
all tuned up and gassed
but something that good
you know ain't gonna last

Just out of the tollbooth
Slim wound it up tight
he was reachin' for second
when on came the light

Now Slim, he's no idiot,
he pulls over quick
and out waddles ol' Jimmy
just wagglin' his stick

Jim walked up to Slim
and looked over the Pan
Slim just sat there smiling
with his papers in his hand

Says Nightstick Jim to California Slim
"I don't like you biker bums,
but I know your papers jive
or else, you would've run

"I keep a quiet stretch of road,"
(that Jim's an ugly cuss)
"next time you plan to come this way
be smart, and take the bus."

Slim, he takes this tirade in
he's quiet, he's no fool
with this cop it'd be a hellatious fight
should ol' Slim lose his cool

Nightstick Jim, he's tough enough
but not known for his wit
he grunts and groans, and pisses an' moans
he don't know when to quit

He rants and raves 'bout hair and beards
and how bikers all have fleases
they never shower, never shave
and have about twelve diseases

Slim, he's heard about enough
and he lights himself a smoke
he looks way up in them beady eyes
and says, "Fatman, you're a joke."

"You got the nerve to tell me
what I can and cannot do?
Let me clue ya straight, Big Jim,
I've got some news for you

"I paid my half a buck to ride
this road, just like the man
in the Lincoln Continental
with the vodka in his hand

"So if you want to write some slips
and get yer little thrills,
go write the drunk in the brand-new cage
or write the guy he kills."

Nightstick Jim, he's heard about enough
and bellows out, "Now listen,
if you don't quit this silly shit
you'll find a few teeth missin'."

"Go ahead," said our man Slim,
"work me over good.
But before you swing, you'd better know
that blood's paid back in blood.

"But if you want to think instead of swing
and listen to my plan
gimme an ear and we'll find out
just who's the better man.

"I've run this road a time or two,
I know its hills and bends
next tollbooth's twenty miles away
that's where the contest ends.

"You in that bright blue cage of yours
and my panhead under me
first one through the tollbooth
decides how it's gonna be.

"If I win," says Slim,
"I ride in peace, and you stay off my back.
If I lose, you can haul my ass away
I won't give you no flak."

Now this sounds pretty good to Jim
as he thinks about various things
but we know that the opry ain't over
'til ya hear the fat lady sing

Nightstick Jim don't say a thing
although he's all enraged
he slides his stick through the big chrome ring
and waddles back to his cage.

California Slim ground out his smoke
and contemplates the ride
Jim turned off his flashin' blues
and pulled up alongside.

"Three even revs, and then we're off!"
called our man Slim to Jim
Nightstick Jim don't say a thing,
he just nods his head at Slim

And side by side they wound 'em up
no one on the road but them
the race of the year is being held here
on the 'pike, at four ayem.

and all the folks
for miles around
slept through the heat
that was comin' down

Between the biker dude
named California Slim
and the monster cop
called Nightstick Jim

They came off the line a-smokin'
in the pale moonlight
the highway patrolman on the left
the biker on the right

The cruiser kicked up into drive
and started to pull away
Slim grabbed third and dropped the clutch
and felt the Panhead sway

At five miles out they were side by side
cruisin' 'bout a hundred and ten
roadside signs loomed large and green
and vanished once again

Slim was glad he had a five-speed
up around a hundred and a half
then the big Dodge started to pull away
you could almost hear Jim laugh

Now Slim's not one to hang it up
when the good times start to go sour
he twisted the wick that last half-inch
and hunched himself down lower

Jammin' through the corners,
cuttin' through the breeze
runnin' flat out, to no avail
slippin' back by degrees

The runners were eighteen miles out
and Slim was runnin' behind
when there came a strange explosion
followed close by a high-pitched whine

Slim, not knowing what it was,
jacked the pan up then and there
in time to see taillights leap to the right
as the cruiser flew into the air

Slim kicked down into second
and pulled over to the bank
to see Nightstick Jim hanging halfway out
of the crushed and crumpled tank

Ya gotta hand it to Jim, thought Slim
That fool can really drive!
"Hey, Nightstick Jim," called out ol' Slim,
"Hey, are ya still alive?"

"I'm livin', Slim," called Nightstick Jim
"but both my legs are broke,
and layin' here in this cloud of gasoline fumes
I think I'm gonna choke."

Now I told you, Slim, he's righteous,
although Jim's just plain no-good
Slim found himself deciding
'tween what he 'ought' and what he 'should'

The easy thing's to ride away
don't even bother to try
after all, he's a miserable sonofabitch
so let his fat ass fry

But that idea didn't set with Slim
'cause he's just not that kind.
after all, it could have been him down there
and Slim made up his mind

And all the folks
for miles around
still wonder about
just what went down

Between the biker dude
named California Slim
and the stove-up cop
called Nightstick Jim

Our man Slim, he spotted the car
and scrambled right down to it
saying, "Hang on, Ace, we'll get you out
but I need some help to do it."

"We're gonna save yer ass tonight,
don't worry about the pain,
but I need a stretch of good stout rope
or a length of heavy chain."

"I know for sure I got no rope,"
Big Jim said through the pain,
"but in the trunk, along with the spare,
I got some tire chains."

Slim checked and found the trunk
had been sprung open in the crash
he pulled out the set of tire chains
and was back in about a flash.

Slim hooked the chains together
and called out, "Hold on tight!
If we do this right the first time,
you'll make it through the night!"

Slim fired up the mighty pan
and snicked it into first
as Nightstick Jim slid up the bank
he knew he'd passed the worst

California Slim pulled Nightstick Jim
up into the breakdown lane
and handed him a flask of rum,
saying, "This'll ease the pain."

As Slim wrapped Jim in his leather coat
Jim looked up and asked, "Why?"
said Slim, "You're a miserable sonofabitch,
but that's no reason to let you die."

And then in the time
it takes to toke
that dead blue cage
went up in smoke

And all the folks
for miles around
to this day don't know
just what went down

Between the biker dude
named California Slim
and his buddy, the cop,
called Nightstick Jim.

Howl at the Moon . . . 'til the Moon Howls Back

J.H. "Colorado T." Sky

got out
hit the road
at dawn's first red crack

full tank
saddlebags
leathers on my back

sunrise
fresh new wind
pocket full of jack

look down
endless road
and never look back

day's end
sun sinks low
shadow stretches back

pull off
light a camp
do some kickin' back

lone wolf
howlin' down
distant darkened track

one guest
eye to I
with a twelve-point rack

small blaze
campfire sings

whispers, pops and cracks

the last
can of beans
from out of my pack

it's here
I belong
And I will be back
To howl
At the moon
'til the moon howls back

to howl
at the moon
'til the moon howls back

I will howl
at the moon. . . .

Cold Summer Night

J. H. "Colorado T." Sky

Dusty tarnished chrome
Glints derisive, chastisive
Flashing Morse messages
From the moon
Through scudding clouds

Nodding within the front porch screen
I start, gasp, sigh
As an arthritic beacon
Signals dewpoint

Joints pop, creak
As my seething apathy
Drives me up

Light a smoke
With my rage

Crack a beer
To quench it

And try to ignore
The persistent, petulant wind
Which all night long
Has called my name

Home Tonight

J. H. "Colorado T." Sky

It's been a long weekend and the time's come to roll on back
I'm out of time, out of luck and my wallet's flat out of jack
I'm a little hungover,
a little stoned-to-the-bone
but like a postal pigeon,
I'll be flyin' on home
Point me in the right direction to get me home tonight

My tank's about empty and my back tire's a little low
my brakelight fuse is cracked and it's ready to blow
I got a bungie wrapped around
where my saddlebag broke
got a bent paperclip
holdin' open my choke
I need a little jerry-riggin' to get me home tonight

My license is expired, but just by a week or two
my insurance ran out and my sticker's way overdue
a little loud in the pipes
but the motor's runnin' nice
oh, Mister State Trooper,
don't ya look at me twice
I need a little bit of luck to get me home tonight

There's something 'bout bein' on the road in the middle of the night
got my knees in the breeze and the world just feels just right
I'll make it on home
if I keep my throttle tight
Like Jerry said,
"before daylight"
I just might get some sleep when I get home tonight

the highway's singin' me a sweet lullaby tonight
along this river of stone 'neath the full moon shinin' bright

it's a little bit of spirit,
a little bit of soul
it's a little bit of rock
and a whole lot of roll
through the night, through the mist, through the pale moonlight
just bein' on my scooter makes it all alright
it's a damn cryin' shame that I gotta go home tonight

Turnabout

J. H. "Colorado T." Sky

There always used to be a lighted pathway
There used to be a candle on the front-room windowsill
There used to be a door, its brass knob warm within my hand
And my name would ride a whisper in the darkness

Now I find the pathway cold and dark and littered
And the unlit candle melted like the detritus of dreams
The walls hold tight the door, the handle useless
And the traces of my footsteps have all vanished from the yard

So now, in silence solemn and despondent
I again commit my spirit to the wind
As the highway sirens sing out to the restless
And the winter comes upon my soul again

In the darkest night a gleam of light can flicker
And a trace of warmth can fend against midwinter's coldest ill
But when a house of hope, once holy, can ignore me
I choose the road and I forsake its boarded chill

A mere building can be bought or burned or bartered
But a house within can truly make an edifice a home
And relations, lovers, children, dogs and breakfast
Can dissuade the impetus to roam

But candles always sputter into puddles
And embers may grow cold upon the hearth
And a shunning shoulder will, for many travellers
Stir the wanderlust that smoulders in their hearts

So tomorrow, in the hour after daybreak
I will make my fond departures at the door
And cinching down the straps on my Matilda
Will dance my highway lover ever more.

Highway Poets (theme poem)

K. Peddlar Bridges

YA!

We're Motorcycle riding
Engine blasting
Line chasing
Gravel chewing
Bug spitting

HIGHWAY . . .   POETS!

YA!

We're Mile driving
Car Passing
Gas burning
Tire Wearing
Muffler roaring
Wind Chasing

HIGHWAY . . .   POETS!

YA!

We're Road cruising
Highway riding
Lane splitting
Line driving
Engine loving
Cop ducking

HIGHWAY . . .   POETS!

YA!

We're Road traveling
Adventure seeking
Mile burning
Horizon chasing
Dream Believing
Life living
Freedom loving

HIGHWAY . . .   POETS!
HIGHWAY . . .   POETS!

        YA!
You got that right!

HIGHWAY . . .   POETS!

Thank You. . . .

If I Only Had a Nickle

K. Peddlar Bridges

If I only had a nickle
For every little town
I ever rode through
Trying to forget
Trying to shake the blues
If I had a nickle
For every time I dialed the phone
And then didn't let it ring
If I only had a nickle
For every Tony's only pizza shop
In every back road town
Where I've sat and stirred coffee
With handle-bar tired hands
And road-wearied and lonely eyes
Ya—if I only had a nickle
For ever old . . . fat-bellied . . . panting-tongued dog—
I've seen run across
. . . a dry yellow lawn
In the twilight of afternoon
. . . setting sun
That reminded me of an old dog once
. . . back home
Ya—if I only had a nickle
For every South Main or Maple Street—
Where I've sat waiting for the light
. . . to change
Not knowing when it did change
Was I going to hook a left or a right
Ya—if I only had a nickle
For every lonely girl's eye I've met
. . . as I've rolled my bike up to the light
Her sitting on a porch or a step
Dreaming of someone coming and
Sweeping her up and taking her away

As my bike idles—our eyes dance
but nobody's got the guts . . .
the gall . . .
or the gumption to make the contact
So when the light turns
Our fate rolls on
But I know there'll be
Another town
Another time
Another girl
Another light
Because—if I only had a nickle
For every girl's eye—every cop's eye
Every punk's eye—
Every cursing driver's eye—
I've steered into
Ya if I only had a nickel
For every cold mile—
Every lonely night
Spent in a damp tent
Under a rainy sky
With un-wanted memories
Like fallen stars and snapping dragons
Singe-ing and nipping at my heart
Ya—if I only had a nickle
For every foot
Every inch
Every mile
I've spent pounding-out
Trying to shake these Blues
Ya—If I had a nickle
For every strangers face
That reminded me of some other strangers
Face—someplace else

If I had a nickle for every little house
That reminded me of some other little
House—someplace else
Ya—if I had a nickle
I'd have a pocketful of dimes
A fistfull of dollars—
But still—
No reason to STOP!

Bikers

K. Peddlar Bridges

Bikers are a strange breed—
Because when it comes to living,
Men act like they're going to live forever
And feel short changed when they don't—
But most bikers know the truth—
When it comes to life
We're all just passing through
So you might as well enjoy the ride—
So—what others measure—
In dollars and cents—
Bikers measure—
in speed and chrome
—cast iron and stainless steel
—black rubber—engine power
And it's what your gauges measure that counts . . .
—Not other's expectations.
It's twisting the wick
Snapping the next gear . . .
Going down the red line
While you streak down the white line.
Leaving all the citizens to stay in line-
'Cause you know the truth
We're all just passing through
And heaven is just one more gear up.

Into the Weirs, Laconia, NH, 2004
(Photo by Michael Lichter)

Laconia Bike Week

K. Peddlar Bridges

Laconia Bike Week
Is the first of the Big Three:
Sturgis . . . Daytona . . . Laconia 1916.

Laconia
Has seen bikes
We have never even known:
Douglases, Dots, Popes and Yales.

Laconia
Has known the Veterans of many Wars:
World War One . . . World War Two
The Korean War—Vietnam—
Desert Storm and now Iraq!

Laconia
has seen Harleys come and go
through the years . . .
The new blocks on the road
Flatheads—Knuckleheads—Panheads
Shovelheads—Evos and now the Twinkies

Laconia
Has known the sparkle of new Harley paint
and the shine of new Harley chrome
and then watched them turn to dull sheen
then rust, then fade away
and then to return again . . . as Retro!

Laconia
Has known the birth of the 60's
Asian Motorcycle Revolution,
has seen Hondas grow from 50cc
single port exhaust

to 1100cc plus engines . . .
with 16 valve power trains.

Laconia
Has known the days of the 80's
When the howl of the Kirker exhaust
was the call of the day
Till the dawn of the new Millennium
when the new V-twin Rumble
took it all back.

Laconia
Has Known
Years with no events,
Years with new events.
It has watched the Track grow
from Back-country Circle
to International Circuit.
It has seen all these events come and go.

Laconia
Has seen
Hill Climbs appear,
then disappear
and then return again;
it has seen the beginnings
of the Big Flea Markets
Custom Bike Shows
Bike Blessings and Rock Concerts

Laconia
Has watched
the Lakeside Crowds grow
from the Hundreds to the Thousands.

Laconia
has watched us age and go
from Young and Wild
to Old and Cool,
and has seen all our changes in between . . .

For Laconia
Has known us all.

That Four-Stroke Song

John Zontar Edwards

Potato potato potato
Makes me yearn
Makes me burn
I want to learn
Why that song does to me
What it does to me.
Potato potato potato potato potato
It makes me yearn.

The Hero

John Zontar Edwards

Children in the back seat stare and
Strange women smile
Little boys run to the road's edge to
Salute and men try to act hard.
Why?
Because everyone needs a hero.
To thumb his nose at death even just for a little while.
I'm that cowboy who rides into the sunset
And they need me.

No Indians

Michael Brown

       at the Susquehanna Art Museum
A Bugatti, a Ducati, and a woman who knew
all about them, museums house things to make us
see in new ways useful things unused:
Electra Glide in blue isolated from film, fans, and rider;
yellow icons cold because sitting is prohibited.
We lean to see through plastic wind screens,
test the leather of fake-looking saddle bags,
long to wrap handlebars in our hands,
tilt the heavy metal, making roars that baffle talk,
sunlight off chrome blinding all but touch,
remembering how it felt at the end of the road.
Twenty-five years ago in the Northwest Territories
a bare-headed man in wraparound shades
and a Cleveland baseball shirt thudded softly
in dusty boots across the porch and into a bar
where we drank whisky and shot pool all afternoon,
not once mentioning the shining dull-red Indian
framed in sunlight outside the open door.
Then the stranger stood astride it,
back wheeled, turned right, kick started,
and disappeared in a rooster tail of dust
down a road no one else had driven all day.
It sticks in the museum of my memory,
big as a Harley standing with gleaming pistons
and lacquered black on blond hard wood
in a small room of the second floor
of the Susquehanna Art Museum.
The gonzo journalist gone.
This Harley not for riding.
No Indians here.

I Gotta Do

Betsy (GypsyPashn) Lister

My wild younger days
are catching up with me
I done gone way past
the age of 53
I'm about as washed up
as a woman could be
But I put on a smile, a smile outside
'Cuz I gotta do what I got to, to ride!

My body aches;
it suffers from the cold
My bones these days
are feeling mighty old
And my muscles now have
a mind of their own
But I don't pay it all no mind
'Cuz I gotta do what I got to, to ride!

My wrist's in a wrap
My hip's in a cast
I done broke my foot,
this summer past
My back's a brace
My arm's in a sling
I'm told I shouldn't do
much of anything
Behind that statement you know
I won't hide
'Cuz I gotta do, what I got to, to ride!

Hell, if I were the tin man
My joints they'd be rust
The rest of me would
Make a nice bronze bust

That's as sedentary as the doc's say
I should be
But they just don't know'
What's goin' on
inside me
So I just take it all in;
all in stride
'Cuz I gotta do, what I got to, to ride.

I've left along the way
Some bodily parts
Some's been donated
To savings the arts
So with what's left
I'll hold onto;
hold onto inside
'Cuz I gotta do, what I got to, to ride.

Liquid libation
gives me duration
And I can wear a brace
and ski mask my face
I can don mittens and woolens
And be all warm inside
'Cuz I gotta do, what I got to, to ride!

Well, on days I be hurting
And feeling a bit ill
I know I can pop me
Another one of them special pills
That sure nuff gonna give me,
Give me the will to survive
'Cuz I gotta do what I got to, to ride!

Well the doc's say I'm pure loco
Done gone lost my sense
Hell, it's like I fell
on the other side of the fence
But I pick myself up
Like a new born bride
'Cuz I gotta do what I got to, to ride!

Well done gone lost my body
And now some say, my mind
People be a talking
And say I'm "that kind"
The type that be crazy
And should be locked up
But I let um know
that I'm just a young pup
And keep them in kind
'Cuz I gotta do what I got to, to ride!

Well you can say
what you want to
Hell; even mean what you say
But I'll just get on my scoot
And ride away
And I won't look back
And with that keep my pride
'Cuz I gotta do what I got to, to ride!

My PHD

Betsy (GypsyPashn) Lister

A connoisseur of motorcycles
I've come to be
It's been a long time coming
Since before I was twenty-three
I've studied the models
Their looks their sizes
Know what makes them look good
How to win those prizes
I'm familiar with most the parts
From the front to the rear
Swing arms, exhaust
And what sounds good to the ear
Recognize the different levers, handlebars and grips
Have scoured the aisles at the local dealerships
Have learned what filters, bolts and nuts
Go on the bike to make it purr when it putts
Know all the light options, the brakes, the wheels
When to shop to get the best of deals
I've memorized the catalogs
And know most the pages
Can customize any model
With the rest of the sages
So now I guess
You can plainly see
While I've been studying and
working on my degree
that Harley-Davidson's
the last two initials
In my P HD

Biking Away from Dooniver

Preston Hood

—for Macdara Woods & the others

We imagined a landscape that included
only what we could bring in our knapsacks.

Some of us could see through the fog beyond the others
so we lead the way up the valley of image
into the hills of sound; some of us even wavered
by twanging too much song. Those that

couldn't voice the words they wanted to say,
went to the ocean, bowed their heads
& paused for a moment, some looked out
all night into starlight to find: a stillness

to center their wavering. The rest of us
followed, drawn into the ritual of silence.
By the sea we heard the others singing
the hallelujah of listening, & with this

the moon tilted with its full-cocked ear:
on the shore by the rocks the waves stopped,
& the dolphins sang their precious song. The moons
luminous light shown down & the sea grew still.

At last, from inside us all, our words came
& we inhaled the sounds of the valley:
the toads croaked, there were crickets, crickets, crickets.
A new voice had brought us to joy.

It's Okay

Susie Howard

It's okay.
It's okay.
It's okay.
The tires revolving down the asphalt
keep saying its okay
leaving behind the mess,
the pain, the thoughts
that travel with me as I walk
haunted by small voices
in the rooms of the house
weighing me down,
always overwhelmed,
anchored.

But the road is free of that
It is the steady air against the skin
whipping hair and clothes
and flawed thinking from my mind
with the steady hum of opposing carburetors
passing by dinosaur Buicks
traveling to destinations of work,
lifestyle, maintenance, dronehood
while I follow no map but that of whim
and its steady song of
It's okay.
It's okay.
It's okay.

WTHEFM

Susie Howard

—for Dr. F.O. No

No, it ain't a radio station,
but I listen to it like its playing my favorite
moldy oldies, yeah,
I know the words, snap my fingers
to its back beat I can use it,
the rhythm of too many days
tuned in or out, a place named
for itself, like "KCUB its a Bear".

No, it ain't the style on my FM dial
I heard over there when home was
far away and dry was a dream cause I sat on my helmet
in the hole, my feet turning to sludge in my boots to
keep the same from happening to my ass,
nodding off to the memory of her
soft thighs, the bow from her bra.

No it ain't the voice from the box,
that bitch, Hot-Jane-Barbarella,
the Stones or little miss
sunshine Hanoi Rose harmonizing
with, "Have decided to
mid-Tet Offensive cease-fire."
Its all beaucoup okay, G.I.,
tallRoundEyeCharlieScreamingEagle.

No it ain't the drone of all the
shitty jobs I've had, been laid
off from, kicked out of, walked
on since I got back till my best
friend is the guy at the Port Authority turnstile
booth who lets me through
for a warm night on the benches,
so long as I move now and then.

No it ain't the sweet sing song of
my kids, scared of me at night when they tried to
climb in my bed but
I freaked out, ready to kill, with
demons before me where my kids
should have been, cause she took
them to hide which was right.

No it ain't the buzz in my brain
when I hear, the 60's—
remember when Little Anthony was Imperial,
when my best friend checks in for methadone treatment,
(after forty years, it ain't
no treatment), when they say,
"Son, you've got PTSD".

No it ain't a radio station.
When in doubt, you got to dance.
Its just a backwards glance.
A trip from then to now.
A long lost life since Hell.
I'm over the comments.
What The Fuck Moments.
Wanna make a request?

The Matador

Jacqueline M. Loring

Desperately trailering our Bultacos
home from the Berkshires
with your new Cyclone,
I listen,
search through sounds
—your moaning,
scraping wipers,
and pelting rain—
for familiar landmarks
to follow

I wish
I'd paid attention
to Dad's directions,
knew my way
to my friend's mountain cabin,
or heard your mother's warning
about my wicked older ways
or knew her better, inside
her kitchen sipping Gold Star tea
with other barefoot Barbie dolls.

I wish
I'd heard the danger
in your father's war stories
of Enduros or Six Day's Trials,
understood his whispered wager
about good stock or first sons to come,
known yesterday
the importance of returning,
uninjured, valued purple hearts,
or could find my own way home.

I do remember
my Nana's fairy tales, lush
green lies of kissing stones, magical
races, prized Grails, pots of gold.
I wish
my mother didn't conjure
images of you shining,
tall on that metal steed,
charging, or frail me,
swooning.
I wish
she'd mentioned mud
and the toll for failing
or how to face your mother,
explain to her this bruised
Matador, you,
half conscious,
in the back seat
of your war-prize Cyclone,
spitting bloody words.

Evolution Amulet

Rev. Martin Jack Rosenblum, a.k.a. "The Holy Ranger"

the 30th Anniversary XLH sat in the dining room
during winter months & once after a late movie
when all slept & the first real snow landed
I got on it & turned the lights toward a
front window shining into the blanket
being tossed upon the birch tree
as winter's comfort & signaling
with yellow flashes reflecting
on an empty television screen:
the first spring rain bringing
this Sportster down the ramp
& across the lawn and sidewalk
to the garage where it
fires up once the carb
swallows ample passion
but the rain keeps any
travel in the alley to
just beads upon fresh
wax or upon the chrome my reflection
while I get down nearer the exhausts
to hear what winter kept in silence.

When There Has Been No Fire

Rev. Martin Jack Rosenblum, a.k.a. "The Holy Ranger"

for some time
  it can usually
    be found traced

          & I consider
          wagontrails or
          paths cut by
          mountain men at

odds with
  wagoneers yet
    ash is the usual

          distance covered
          & this can be felt
          as I shove my hands
          beneath   the leaves &

entirely   past
  the waist of
    her slip   .

Enter
(From The Last Autumn Ride)

Rev. Martin Jack Rosenblum, a.k.a. "The Holy Ranger"

the scattered leaves
against the side
of the garage

wet from
an afternoon
rain this fall
the slight wind
in later afternoon
light qualities   :
images receding
from cut edges

into burnt ridges
against a backlit
storm door entry.

The Blues

Rev. Martin Jack Rosenblum, a.k.a. "The Holy Ranger"

This gets played in twelve-bar progressions
on my old 12-string with its cherry sunburst
radiating notes that hit   the morning sun just
like drops of rain on the backyard grass   stepped
upon unmowed & stained where the dog squats to mark
his spot we all later sit with beer cans tucked into
the velvet guitar case which mats the grass   like a coffin
would the earth for once we're done all we'll hear is the
blues muffled harking &   splitting the night that drops in

.

Wisconsin Winds

Rev. Martin Jack Rosenblum, a.k.a. "The Holy Ranger"

Wisconsin winter crowds the roads
cutting the center line & wrapping
the shoulders
then off into the fields fenceposts
stick up as reminders
of spring's territory
& the blackbirds upon
those telephone wires
call to winter's
attention that
they aren't being scattered by
the holy exhaust roar from the

Harley Sportster that is restrained
by vinyl covering & plastic-coated
chains upon an insulated board in
a garage that is visited late at
night when the house is tight &
the yard flushed by the light
coming from my office window
where the walls are covered
with pictures of motorcycle

Kabbalah: the Old Iguana wearing
a shoulder rig in the bog
the ivory grips like open
April sunlight
Willie G. shaking hands
on a hot June afternoon
the front mudflap made
from carriage leather by
Hunt's Harness on one
visit to Colgate in
summer's late heat

the Holy Ranger
firing a Buntline Special
at rogue soda cans along
the road to the Monches
dump having dismounted
to take care of the
situation before it
got out of hand
the Gibson found in a
sixties ecstasy still
strung for trouble
in its hardshell
battered from
barroom blues

—these offroad memories found in
frames to contain their snowbound
imagery that develops further an
instant after Wisconsin spring on
the roads cutting about evolution
power drifts like so many friends
in the continuous Midwestern wind

SCREAM LOUD

RatLizard Smith

—in memory of Rob Bridges

Scream loud, the road is a cruel lover.
she takes life and limb; leaves only feelings
as you suffer and recover.
she calls aloud to you again.

Scream loud, the road is a cruel lover.
open and inviting, ready to devour
the meat of your body through leather armor.

Scream loud, the road is a cruel lover.
even if you never left her, all you want is more.
gritting teeth, rushing wind, give life to the soul.

Try to scream!
sparks fire up the darkness as you hug her body.
asphalt orgasm, give no less
to that love so badly wanted.

SILENCE!
blood and oil, you bleed together.
the road is a cruel lover.

Flip Side Me

Eddie "Sorez the Scribe" Pliska

Childhood filled
With violence
On one side
Of the flipside
Of that coin
Tales
Love and bandages
Heads
So filled with love
And violence
Is who I am
Take a chance
Flip that coin
If it lands standing
Upon its side
Then you have found
The true me

Life's Highway

Eddie "Sorez the Scribe" Pliska

Past littered with baggage
Darkness enveloped my soul
Showed to all I did not care
Out there on the road
In my prime at the time
Or so I must have thought
Older now looking back
Respect is what I sought
This highway called life
A hard row to hoe
Especially when
You choose life on the road
Respect earned deserved
With blood, sweat and tears
My presence was known
My wrath was feared
Hardcore now softened
By thousands of miles
A greybeard now
A greybeard who smiles

Uneasy Rider

Diane Wakoski

Falling in love with a mustache
is like saying
you can fall in love with
the way a man polishes his shoes
        which,
        of course,
        is one of the things that turns on
        my tuned-up engine

        those trim buckled boots

        (I feel like an advertisement
        for men's fashions
        when I think of your ankles)

Yeats was hung up with a girl's beautiful face

and I find myself

a bad moralist,

a failing aesthetician,

a sad poet,

wanting to touch your arms and feel the muscles
that make a man's body have so much substance,
that makes a woman
lean and yearn in that direction
that makes her melt/she is a rainy day
in your presence
the pool of wax under a burning candle
the foam from a waterfall

You are more beautiful than any Harley-Davidson
She is the rain,
waits in it for you,
finds blood spotting her leg
from the long ride.

The Desert Motorcyclist

Diane Wakoski

Road as wide open
as my shoulders when I am loving
the tides
the dry sand that blows against you like rain—
I am riding away from you;
away from your voice that troubles me,
like a leak in the basement,
away from your timidities
about frogs and salamanders,
away from this desert road,
purple and bloody with dusk.
Pools of the afternoon spray me,
distorting your image.
You caged me in water,
imprisoned me in tide pools/remembering I am the spiny starfish,
softer inside than evolution should allow.

Now I run away
to my dry desert,
the place where there is enough space
for my imagination
and nothing to drown it.

Desert motorcyclist:
that is me.
And it is the man,
never the machine
who betrays me.

Wondering Aloud: Several Haiku

Wu Hai "Woo Wu" Tien,
Regional Secretary, HPMCC Pacific Rim Chapter, Hong
Kong

(with thanks to Ian Anderson for the title)

Beyond wondering
To dare to risk finding out
"Intellectuum"

• • •

defeat inertia
dance into inspired action
let your conscience lead

• • •

truth, punctuating
with comma fangs, will bite you
in the asterix

• • •

mind kept clear, heart right,
well prepared: one never knows
when tsunami comes

Abuckandaquarter

Terry Rozo

I pulled in the clutch and with a twist of the wrist and a tap of my toe, the bike kicked into gear. I leaned back and took it all in. The crimson sky of the setting sun played backdrop to the Race Point Lighthouse. I rode on up to the crest of a hill, you know, the one between the Visitors Center, the airport, and the Atlantic Ocean. My body went into automatic pilot; my brain into its right side and with that, a flood of images ran through my mind.

There I was during the summer of '86 at Herring Cove, b-b-q-ing chicken and drinking red wine at sunset, alone.

Me driving up to Provincetown in '82 in my beat-up, faded, light blue Volkswagen Beetle. It was right after my breakup with Denise, windows half-open, the rain dripping onto the tattered Road Atlas that laid in the empty passenger seat, while I cried the whole drive up from NYC. My box of tissues being emptied and sent swirling around the inside of the VW by the wind.

Into the Race Point parking lot and right back out. I was off towards Herring Cove on a long stretch of road where I could hit 90mph.

"Terry, I gotta tell you," now I'm flashing back to the summer of '87. I'm living with Diana and her 15 year old, Paula for the summer while I worked at the magazine. Diana is out of town for the weekend and I'm the babysitter, "Terry, I gotta tell ya, we were doing a buck and a quarter last night on Route 6, I was sitting in the back seat thinking how bad you would feel if something happened to me, I'll never do that again." I thought that was a cool thing for her to say.

It was night, I rode past the back of the Cove, and open throttled towards the breakwater, changed my mind, hung a left onto Bradford, and rode into town.

Highway Poets & Friends
Photo Section

Poet Gerald Stern with José Gouveia
(PHOTO BY SARA O'ROURKE – 2008)

Cowboy poet Jeff Streeby with José Gouveia
(Photo by Annalies Zijderveld – 2007)

Marc (Moshe) Goldfinger, Betsy (GypsyPashn) Lister,
and K. Peddlar Bridges
(Photographer unknown – 2008)

J. Barrett (Bear) Wolf
(PHOTO BY COLETTE MCCURRY – 2007)

Betsy (GypsyPashn) Lister
(PHOTO BY BILL GRASSIA – 2007)

Susan Buck
(PHOTO BY WILLIAM RADACINSKI – 2007)

Martin Jack Rosenblum
(Photo by Daniel De Lone)

K. Peddlar Bridges
(Photo by Michael Lichter – 2007)

José (JoeGo) Gouveia, Dennis Brutus, and Colorado T. Sky
(Photo by Chase Berggrun – 2008)

John "Zontar" Edwards
(Photo by Sandy Nicole Medeiros – 2008)

Anne Marie Macari, J. Barrett (Bear) Wolf, Poet Gerald Stern,
José Gouveia, Colorado T. Sky
(Photo by Sara O'Rourke – 2008)

Colorado T. Sky, Betsy (GypsyPashn) Lister, and K.Peddlar Bridges
(Photo by Susan Buck – 2007)

Colorado T. Sky
(Photo by José (JoeGo) Gouveia – 2008)

J. Barrett (Bear) Wolf
(Photo by Don Rauschmeier – 2007)

Biker Poetry is more. . . .
MarySusan Williams-Migneault

Biker Poetry is more . . .
than images on a page
more powerful than . . .
the Spoken Word of Slam or Rant or Rap.
Biker Poetry is the engine firing up
blasting across the horizon
stretching out before you   waiting.
It is the gravel in your pores
the bugs up your nose
the rain scraping your skin
as it whizzes across your face
the sun setting while the engine cools
and you sit staring out a diner window—
admiring your steel pony while breaking bread
with your Biker brothers or sisters
Biker Poetry is the breath . . .
the soul . . . of a spirit
that chases after the wind
and calls the "Road" home.

The Ride: Into the Flame

MarySusan Williams-Migneault

Every muscle in her belly
strained to hold her steady,
while the energy of his body
leaned into the wind
and drew her into his flame—
The thickness of his fingers
slid her legs nearer to his hips.
The chill of autumn's air stole her breath
as the steady vibration of the engine
stirred her blood, intoxicated her soul.
As if one with their Harley stallion,
they glided through Essex farmlands,
on Old-New-England country-roads.
Nature's foreplay teased their senses.
Their metal steed's tires kissed
each narrow twist and turn.
"Hang on, darlin.." he warned,
then cut the wheel off-road. . . .
Their bodies banged, bounced up,
then smashed right back down;
their boots found the foot-pegs,
pushed hard and stood straight up.
Her arms locked around his waist,
heart pounded against her chest.
Her breath froze in mid-air, and yet,
from deep inside her gut
she heard herself yell out:
"Don't stop. . . . Not now. . . . Not ever!"

Cowboy and Biker

Laurence P. Scerri, a.k.a. "Ironhorse Writer"

Cowboy and Biker
A long, dusty road
Dismounted respective saddles
In an effort to unload

"Where ya headin'?" says Cowboy
Biker gave a stare
"Wherever my kickstand sets to rest
That's when I know I'm there"

Both men spoke of rides long past
Of those yet still beyond
Of horse, horse power, helmet and hat
A handshake being their bond

How lives resigned to freedom's fight
Accept all consequences
How those forsaking freedom's blood
Accept a life of fences

Biker pulled out a well-worn flask
Two swigs were left, at most
Told the Cowboy, "One's for you
I propose we drink a toast"

"Here's to the ladies, pure as day
Who tried to steer us right
Here's to those who made it hard
The ladies of the night"

"Here's to bein' right with God
Learnin' from mistakes
To fixin' all the wrong ya can
Doin' what it takes"

A deep voiced drawl bellowed, "Amen"
A leather vested, "Righteous" replied
As a long, dusty trail beckoned once more
For a Cowboy and Biker to ride

Writers of the Asphalt Range

Laurence P. Scerri, a.k.a. "Ironhorse Writer"

—for all those who ride and and write

An unfurling road
As a turning page
Feeds the soul
Sets the stage

Within each town
Beyond the bend
A destiny scribed
Upon the wind

Steel reins
Hooves of chrome
Pen to paper
Bring it home

The 'Ridden' word
Their common bond
A seed within
That grows beyond

Righteous wanderers
Refusing change
Writers of
The Asphalt Range

Kin in the Wind

Laurence P. Scerri, a.k.a. "Ironhorse Writer"

A greybeard biker
A white-muzzled mutt
A side car scoot
Named, 'Three Legged Putt'

Bedroll, dog bowl
Jerky to share
A squint, a pant
Off to anywhere

Two old dogs
Kin in the wind
One beyond tricks
The other beyond sin
Howlin' at the moon
Pickin' off fleas
Chasin' life
Faces in the breeze

Nature calls
All too abrupt
Its gear kicked down
Hind leg up

Off the highway
An old dirt road
Biker and dog
In kickback mode

"We're burnin' daylight"
Said with a grin
Off to anywhere
Once again

Two old dogs
Kin in the wind
The bond of Freedom
Burns within
Chasin' life
Is all they need
A heritage born
Of an American Breed

First Gear

Panhead Josh

First Gear
Anger Floods
My Veins

Second Gear
Tears Start To Flow
As I Pull Away

Third Gear
The Wind
Drys My Tears
But The Pain
Won't Go Away

Fourth Gear
Where Should I Go?
Why Should I Stay?

Fifth Gear
All Becomes A Blur
I'm On My Last Nerve

I'm Out Of Gears
But You're Still
On My Mind
I Crack The Wick

Listen To
The Bike Whine
With Thoughts Of You
Still On My Mind

Indian Larry (1949-2004)
PHOTO BY SUSAN BUCK, NYC – 1997

I knew Larry for over 10 years. I always admired his commitment to the purist's philosophy of choppers, though I never quite understood his affection for hardtails, given the quality of NYC pavement. He always respected my rides, and my affection for such ornaments as shock absorbers and saddlebags. We shared a deep love of New York, from Coney Island to The Thousand Islands.

In his single years, Larry's gentlemanly charm was undeniable. But he was as respectful as a man could be, especially when I called to pick his brains. It was a priceless gift.

I could ask Larry a serious question about the meaning of biker symbolism, and get an answer loaded with worldly culture. He was no less savvy on technical matters, like welding or frame geometry. Yet he was also unpretentious enough to admit when he didn't know or understand, and grateful to learn.

Renaissance Man wasn't a catchy label he used, he was a brilliant, eccentric, intelligent, creative, and deeply spiritual soul. He had a lot left to teach us. I'll really miss him.

—*Susan Buck, September, 2004*

Indian Larry, from a Friend to a Friend

Don Clady

Dedicated to my friend Indian Larry for we shared many the same dream. Now my friend, ALL the winds are yours and the roads wide open, like only you could want them to be . . . until we meet again, and we will.

To understand the following, is to know the man.

Vengence Is Mine Said The LORD!

WORDS. . . . What words could I give to you,
to make this saddened day, go beyond
and back a few, then maybe we would say . . .

I knew a man so seemingly,
first glance I did not know, a kinder,
simpler dreamer with an endless depth in soul.

He touched so many closely,
never forgetting where he's been.
He'd treat all so specially and to each brought back a friend.

Way back when he was simply, just a dreamer of a dare,
he stood amongst the Best of them, without a single fear.

The Reaper called him harshly, and the man he would reply:
I deal NOT the reaper's way . . . and you know my reason why!!!!!

And he said: "If you build it, you can come!"   And He Did. . .
.

I Am Into the Ride

Susan Buck

One the first night warm enough to ride without a leather
When a crescent moon hangs in a humid, blue velvet sky
I am into the ride, baby,
I'm just into the ride.

The black asphalt urban expressway is lit up like indoors
with tall, long-necked aluminum street lights
and yellow LED signboards popping out
against the flashing red tail lights of the cars I'm passing.
I am into the ride, man,
I'm just into the ride.

The serene quiet of everything except my engine wailing at the top of
fourth gear,
but knowing there's not open enough road to wind out fifth . . .
I am into the RIDE,
I am INTO the ride.

The heat of the engine is perceptible at 50 miles an hour,
in about 75 degrees of June
I just kick back and open my knees to a little more breeze
I am into the ride, man,
I'm just into the ride.

Then it all gets so smooth, even if the road waves up and down hill,
The trees and retaining walls and corporate crackerbox palaces and
city brownstones
fly by as thought I'm sitting still in a moving road,
not cruising in the saddle of my Super Glide
I am into the ride, baby,
I'm just into the ride.

The red tail lights in front of me and the white tail lights in the
opposite direction disappear for a split second with each bend,

like I've run out of road,
then the road returns
I am into the ride, baby,
I'm just into the ride.

Heading west on the Grand Central, the world's most beautiful
skyline
growing clearer on my city-lit horizon
Airplanes approaching LaGuardia seem to scrape the top of my
helmet
yet at speed, I'm barely buffeted by the wind.
I'm sooo diggin' this ride, man,
I'm really diggin' the ride.

Snaking through traffic, swerving around potholes and tar snakes
like a self-propelled pinball never hitting the bumpers,
and hitting the jackpot is landing safe in my own driveway
'cause then I get to do it all over again.
I am into the ride, baby,
I'm just here to ride.

Rain Poem

Susan Buck

I'm rarely the first to complain
I have a biker's high threshold of pain
But when Mère Nature pulls the plug and the skies do drain
Over city and village; mountain, valley, or plain,
I simply prefer to refrain
From riding my motorcycle in the rain.

For a couple of hours, I felt pretty brave
But my boots have soaked through, and there's no way I can wave
This highway's so bad that it's practically unpaved
The potholes and roadkill turn tunnels to caves
Between semi's and SUVs, another close shave
Other drivers must think I'm completely depraved
It's sunshine and smooth roads that I honkin' crave!

The windshield is cloudy with puddles and stains
My faceshield's steamed up, I'm bent like a crane
In water-soaked gloves, my fingers are stained
My slicker has leaked, I'm chilled to the vein
So, I hold fast to my iron pony's reins
Challenging all of my body and brain

Every twist in the road is a zen riding test
Each gust of wind is firmly addressed
It blows north by northeast, yet I stay the course west
Skidding of wheels—carefully repressed
Rain-soaked disc brakes should never be stressed
Through drizzle and downpour I do not digress

Wet-weather driving skills, they can't even feign
Ferrchrissakes, you moron, get out of my lane!
(Well, usually, that'd come out way more profane)
You think that my wits are a little unchained?
Declare me insane to traverse wet terrain?

To reach home, thirty more miles remain

For all of the valuable experience I gain
I'd almost consider a plane or a train
But from this adventure how could I abstain?
So in weather both wet and mudane,
Rubber side down, I'll sustain
And by the power I draw from octane
I'll ride till the tank is drained.

Rubberband

Susan Buck

I draw my hair back, out of my eyes,
and pull the pony tail through the rubber band
Later, you pull it from my hair, letting it fall,
long, loose over my face, my shoulders,
then gently remove a tendril from my lips
and kiss me . . .

as refreshing as pulling my hair off my neck on a hot summer day
taking that rubber band off my wrist to bind it.
I remove the band in the shower,
toss it in the box of barretts and clips and headbands.
Months later, it's all stretched out
and can't remember how to hold my hair any more
and on a cold autumn day
I still want you to kiss me.

The Shovel Poem

Preacher

A Shovel's my ride,
I built him with pride,
with care for my trusted old friend.
We been through the clubs,
the law and its rubs,
and together we'll be to the end.

He's been a dresser, a rigid,
He's a softail now, to help soothe my "gettin old bones."
Don't matter what He's in,
cause since 1981 He's been,
My Shovelhead and always will be.

There are newer and faster,
and sleeker and such,
but I don't care for that stuff that much.
I like what I like,
and I built what I ride,
with an old friend my Shovel,
that I still ride with pride.

So you ride your V-Rod, your Evo, 2Cam,
you are who you are, and I am who I am,
Know that I'll wave from my shovel,
when we pass on the road,
For what you ride, I dont really care,
cause what it's REALLY about,
is just being out there.

These Cobwebs Gotta Go!

Dick Epstein

I found my gloves, waterproofed
my leathers and my old tanker boots.
I leaned her over to check the oil.
Gave her full choke. She cranked
right up. She was waiting for me.

As I ride down Capitol View,
a soccer mom in her station wagon
throws a cigarette out of her window.
A dump truck spills wet leaves
as we turn a tight corner. Then
I swerve to avoid an old pickup truck
that suddenly appears in front of me.
All of this on one short stretch
of Capitol View.

As we reach the ramp to 495
we lean hard into the turn and
pick up speed as we head west
toward the Blue Ridge.

At 3500 rpm she yawns at 55.
At 4500 she smiles at a smooth 65.
As we hit 75 I back off the gas.
She lets out a groan.

At 5500 we've run out of road.
She wants to go. At 6000 she screams
with delight. My soul says go,
but my brain says no. We're doing

105 with an adrenaline flow.
The sun, a winding road,
and a responsive machine
is all we need.

The State Trooper & the Biker Get Tested

Marc D. "Moshe" Goldfinger

I still remember taking my first motorcycle license
test. It was February, 1967, and the temperature was
17 degrees out.

Having already passed the written test a few weeks
ago, which unlike today, was on a paper that was
handed in to a human police monitor, I rode in,
nervous but determined to pass. The motorcycle I was
riding was a two-stroke 305cc 1965 Yamaha. The
motorcycle I had waiting at home was a 441cc BSA,
single-cylinder 4-stroke with an ultra-high
compression. It was running loud and ugly so I knew
it wasn't the bike to bring in for the test.

The motor vehicle inspector examined my paperwork.
"Anyone who comes out in weather like this to take a
motorcycle test knows how to ride," he said.

It was an assumption on his part but it worked to my
advantage. Maybe he just wanted to get back inside;
maybe he was a nice guy; maybe the unknown.

He pointed to the motorcycle course, then said,"Just
ride around it once, no fancy stuff, and get back
here."

I did what he said and when I got back, he handed me
the paperwork to get my license.

"Be careful out there," was what he said.

Many years later, having lost all my driving rights
for many years for various nefarious activities, in
May of 2004, I rode in to the Massachusetts Office of

Motor Vehicles to take my riding test, having already passed the written test which, if I remember correctly, consisted of 40 simple questions flashed on a computer screen, multiple choice.

I was 58 years old now. The Massachusetts State Trooper looked me over. Here I was, a grey-bearded hippie-type looking guy riding a beat-up 1985 Honda Rebel 250cc 4-stroke, all original stock except for the mirrors, dents in the tank and all.

He put his finger on one of the dents.

"Been down?" he asked.

"No," I replied. "This was my wife's bike and I just put it back on the road so I could ride again."

He asked me to show him the hand signals for right turn, left turn, and stop and, because I was nervous, at first I showed the right turn for the left, and didn't show the proper sign for stop for a second, and then said, "Oh, I forgot," and showed the proper sign.

He looked at me sternly. "Improper use of signals fails you automatically. You'll have to take the test again.

"But tell me, why are you learning on your wife's bike?"

I told him. My wife had died of a drug overdose in 1998 and I inherited it. I had been riding from 1967 up until 1987, when I lost my license because of a number of offenses related to drugs.

"How are you doing now?" he asked. "You look pretty healthy for someone who used drugs."

I explained that I had gotten clean in 1994 and that was when my wife and I separated. I had taught her how to ride in 1986.

"So you haven't been riding since 1987?"

"Well," I said,"I haven't ridden since 1993, to be honest."

His eyes sparked in the sun as he tilted up his mirror-sunglasses and looked at me for a long minute.

"Show me those hand signals again," he said, and I got them right this time. I knew I had failed and was resigned to coming back. Acceptance of what was actually happening was the key to emotional success. Sometimes I could make it work for me.

"Okay, take the bike out for a spin around the parking lot and weave through those stanchions I have set up over there," he said.

I took it out, putting the on the blinker as I pulled out, and cruised the course with ease. I know how to ride. I pulled back over to him, using the stop signal.

"You know," he said, "I think I'm going to pass you. You obviously know how to ride and I can tell you've had a hard road. It's not my job to make it any harder."

He handed me the paperwork and I thanked him.

He said, "Just a minute. I want you to know that the roads have changed alot since you last rode. They're not friendly anymore, so look out for the other guy. They won't be looking out for you."

I looked at him and nodded my head, said thanks again.

"You seem like a good guy. I hope things stay good for you."

As I went back into the Motor Vehicle Agency I thought about that state trooper. I remembered all the bad experiences with police, but I couldn't get this guy out of my mind. "I guess they're not all bad, eh," I thought.

Two assessments had taken place that day. He'd passed me and I'd passed him. I rode out of the parking lot with my motorcycle license in my pocket, riding legal for the first time in over ten years.

Your Tribe

Mary Carol Kennedy a.k.a. "Songbird"

You've invited me into your tribe. . . .
Who are these characters?
I'm Terrified!
The only bikes I have are two model replicas . . .
that sit in square boxes collecting dust on the mantle.
Yes, I want to ride, as I strap on my helmet.
Yes, I want to be, the Songbird Bikerpoet.
Yes, I want to wear leather from head to toe,
and to understand what it means to be an ol' lady...
Let's Go!!
Yes, to ride with you, partner,
Who feels and appreciates . . .
My breath on your neck,
and my hands 'round your rib cage.
Yes, to be a freedom rider,
With thousands of others,
who are out-laws, sisters, kin, friends, and brothers.
Yes, to say, here I am with my ol' man and his Harley.
We live and love today because we gave up the barley.
God, thanks to this biker who still has a heart.
He is more than a tin man.
He's got the key that says . . .

START!!

Burn Out

Kate Johnson a.k.a. "Chopper Kate"

Light it up and burn it!
Excitement builds
like the white hot smoke
the faster you turn it.
Friction is born
as the asphalt bites
and rubber's torn,
powdered and shredded.
Deep and dark
you leave a black mark
that stays forever
here embedded
like ground tattoos
that say, "You earned it!"
Go ahead son,
make your mark
on this world!
For objects that spin
are meant to be hurled
back to the wind.
Sounds and smells
carried away on the breeze,
but a burn out makes an impression
that never leaves.

The "Cycle" of Life
Kate Johnson a.k.a. "Chopper Kate"

Back in the day
weren't you somethin' to see!
Coveted, revered
Hey, Look at me!
Katrillions, gazillions
of tiny bits of dust
collecting in cracks
creeping into crevices
your just,
battered and barraged
over countless miles
sucking endless wind
your luster, lack and lost,
the wheel of time
collects the toll
a heavy metal cost.
You old school
icon of the past
move aside!
Make way for the new
the cool!
More shine, more gears,
the years,
moving way too fast.
Parts worn and stressed
by constant demands
those pistons compressed
enough air to inflate
all those fabled lead balloons!
Your used and abused
now abandoned to rust!
Life is just a "cycle",
ashes to ashes
dust to dust.

Real Bikers Never Cry

Neil Cotter

I did 500 miles today
To get a cheeseburger with the guys
No, I'm not crying
It's just something in my eyes

Tommy bought cheap goggles
It's like everything he buys
Now he looks like a raccoon
Two black rings around his eyes

I got whacked on my scoot
"Was it your fault? No lies."
No baby I was good.
The cager had closed eyes.

Might never ride again
Lifelong severed ties
No, I'm not crying
I think something's in my eyes

Lost three friends that same year,
all on different rides.
They were here, now they're gone,
time not on their sides.

I'll take it on the chin
and take what time buys
but I'm sure gonna miss
Sunday rides with those guys

I'll always turn my head,
when I hear a twin roar by
Nothing else trips my trigger
No matter what I try

Sometimes I hear the bikes leaving
Early with the sun rise
No, I'm not crying
It's just something in my eyes

Thirteen Voyagers

Patricia Hope

Thirteen Voyagers
Carve space through
Evergreen passes
Roads ending
In Rhododendron and
Million-year-old mountains

Little Man

Titus Waalwijk, a.k.a. "Zwerver"

I am caught on the highway
Eternally guarded
By my love for freedom.
Here in the saddle I am
Master of my life.

You are everywhere along the road
Looking frightened
When I pass by
Silently jealous of the ride
I must have had.

What you really saw
Was a dust cloud I left behind.
Wrapping around the story
You will tell later in your local bar
About that angel in
The dust cloud.

Sturgis 1969

Ibunda

She wears flowers in her hair
A look at absent-minded and infinite love
It's a long road

"Do you want a cigarette?"

She asks me

And her eyes look sultry
When I offer her a light

She grabs my hand, vibrates a bit
At the touch of hot skin
In black leather

We inhale smoke
Feel connected to the unwitting future

That should bring no action
But everything

"How much longer," she asks me

I look at her—not understanding
She smiles, her white teeth exposed
Repeats her demand

"Just how long"

The road is long and indeterminate
But freedom makes its niche
As long as you don't enter the path shackled
You don't have to know where it ends

Her sigh is as a light wind, even shines

There is something in her eyes
When she slightly touches my soft cheek and says:

"Ride to live but don't live to ride,
there are many road trips to heaven"

I grin at her once:

"Hey honey, I'm a cowboy
wanted for my sins"

Baiku

Ibunda

Old black leather hands
they just cursed my way of life
it's hard to ride on

Seems like yesterday
the hot road shines beneath wheels
where tomorrow lives

Live the ride of life
sometimes it's impossible
to live on a road

Whenever it shines
between the wheels of thunder
life will glow again

It's my dirty mind
the black leather buddyseat
takes me everywhere

Somehow it takes me
down under hot steel and wheels
I truly like it

How does it take me
the wind blowing in my hair
it just takes me on

Wherever you go
blowing in a dusty wind
your road will follow

Ain't no mountain high
to ride the ride of my life
it's just breath taking

Dirty Little Secret
Debra Coppinger Hill

While other teen-age girls
dressed in cookie-cutter pleated skirts,
with clutch-purses of allowance,
stormed the mall in gaggles,
sighing over frilly dresses,
pining over shiny accessories,
plotting perfect prom nights,
and giggling about boys. . . .

I hid my dirty little secret,
in jeans and a worn thin bandana,
trying to be inconspicuous
as I stared into the window
at the local bike shop
and lusted
for black leather chaps . . .
and wings.

As they dressed proper,
styled their hair like Farrah,
attended cotillion and senior tea,
all the while kissing-up
to eligible boys' parents;
I passed wrenches, read Easy Rider
and snuck midnight rides
clinging to the backs of guys
of "disreputable reputation."

Gaggle-Girls married and settled down,
raised dull clone-like children
and forced smiles over cocktails
as they lied "I'm so happy."
I just heard tell,
I wasn't there.

I was kept out.
I was not 'in.'

I saw the world on two wheels,
ten thousand miles at a time,
lived the adventures I dreamed
and breathed true freedom.
At 30, slowed down enough for kids,
who clung behind me,
who relished my biker-gal tales,
and lived their own adventures.

I acquiesced to a pleading friend,
attended the class reunion,
hid-out in the ladies room,
was accosted by two old gaggle-girls.
Though they never spoke in the past,
they shared that secretly
they admired my courage,
envied my fearless free spirit.

One divorced and living on alimony,
the other the wife of an attorney,
they questioned me about my life
as it was . . . as it is.
Asked what kind of machine to buy,
what clothes to wear,
where to go and what to see
and what it takes to be a 'biker-babe.'

I could be brutal, tell them
"It's just not happening",
instead I offer suggestions
that they note in Blackberries;

They will rush out and buy it all,
"oooh & aaah" like they did back then,
over shiny earrings and dresses
used to lure the boys in.

They'll deck out to the nines,
'ride like the wind',
careful to keep their speed
below the legal limit.
Bikes will fill the void
left vacant by missing adventure,
all eventually falling into storage
where all fads are kept.

Neither will ever be
a Biker Chick.
That title is not for sale
at any shop in the mall.
The band plays 70's tunes,
"Born to Be Wild" blares out.
I laugh . . . my dirty little secret,
is now the height of fashion.

Concrete Cowboy
Debra Coppinger Hill

He was born too late to be,
      what he knows he is in his soul,
And though he's quite accomplished,
      sometimes he doesn't feel quite whole.

He's a lawman of sorts,
      born out of his time,
Trying to uphold basic beliefs,
      an example of toeing the line.

And he rides an iron horse,
      though it's not a muscled steed,
It gets him where he's going,
      when ever there's a need.

They say, sometimes he's crazy,
      plumb out of his mind,
Searching, for something,
      they say he'll never find.

He rides the asphalt prairie,
      through the heat and the cold,
Just a Concrete Cowboy,
      in search of Days of Old.

He believes in rescuing maidens,
      broken down beside the road,
And he wouldn't have it any other way,
      than to live by the Code...

"Do what's right by every man,
      and never compromise,
Be good to little children,
      'cause life is a surprise."

Stuck between buildings,
       of metal, brick and glass,
The only time he sees green pastures,
       is when he cuts the grass.

Looking for a way out,
       to a place deep in his dreams,
Only other Cowboys,
       would ever know what he means.

When he says he's headed someplace,
       where he'll race the open sky,
Only other Cowboys,
       understand the reason why...

Why he rides an Iron Horse,
       for all the world to see,
It's his one last chance to go back,
       to a time when he was free.

Loyal in his heart,
       to those gone before,
He scans the horizon,
       looking for that open door.

In the company of Ghost Riders,
       in the roaring of engine and wind,
He searches for his destiny,
       old lovers and old friends.

Galloping across the miles,
       one day he'll reach the open sky,
Many, will see him pass,
       but only other Cowboys will sigh,

And join him on Iron Horses,
      through time reflected in the glass,
Riding towards the future,
      in an effort to reach the past.

To be Uplifted

Cecil Plaatjies, HPMCC National Secretary, South Africa

O' yeo' yeo', N'gi D'ha!

Rejoice! Rejoice!
We have eaten!
Victory!
I, you, we, o' yeo' yeo'

Come now the festive,
    in rejoicing eat of the meat of the road,
    drink of the wine of the mind sing of the poem
    of the wind live the life that fears no death except the death
of apathy

Ya i'i, Ya i'i!

Come now the grateful, in rejoicing
Dance the world that rolls beneath your wheels
See all there is, behold, enjoy
Learn all there is, imbibe, delight
Teach all you know, impart, rejoice
Share the world that rolls within your mind
U'ehohi m'dala, U'eho shampeti
To do godly deeds is to walk among the gods.

O' yeo' yeo', N'gi D'ha!

i'm chopper wired baby

blaze elliott

i'm a fifties model baby
i got class and i got style
i got chrome and i got rubber
come ride on me a while

ain't no fancy wire harness
as runs this slick machine
i'm chopper wired baby
kick me over make me scream

throw yer leg across me baby
where do ya feel my thunder
i'm low and lean and mean
i'm a bobtailed lightnin wonder

i been stretched and i been lowered
i been dropped and i been rode
it's been fifty years of highway baby
but i ain't feelin old

i'm a fifties model baby
drop yer ass down on my seat
squint yer eyes and hang on tighter
feel my howlin blue chrome heat

i'm a hardtail model baby
for yer hard ridin predilection
you crave the way i tear you up
high octane fueled addiction

ride me til yer shakin baby
ride me til we're dry
i'm an old school little badass bitch
so come give me a try

First Party at Ken Kesey's with Hell's Angels

Allen Ginsberg

Cool black night thru the redwoods
cars parked outside in shade
behind the gate, stars dim above
the ravine, a fire burning by the side
porch and a few tired souls hunched over
in black leather jackets. In the huge
wooden house, a yellow chandelier
at 3 A.M. the blast of loudspeakers
hi-fi Rolling Stones Ray Charles Beatles
Jumping Joe Jackson and twenty youths
dancing to the vibration thru the floor,
a little weed in the bathroom, girls in scarlet
tights, one muscular smooth skinned man
sweating dancing for hours, beer cans
bent littering the yard, a hanged man
sculpture dangling from a high creek branch,
children sleeping softly in their bedroom bunks.
And 4 police cars parked outside the painted
gate, red lights revolving in the leaves.

Afterword

Rubber Side Down Or Shiny Side Up!

It's hard to write an afterword for something that is still in full flight forward, but that is just what I have been asked to do. No one can point to the main taproot of the Bikerpoetry tree. No one can point to the exact moment that Bikerpoetry became a spirit in its own right rather than an offshoot of another plant. It is easily believed now that Bikerpoetry is an entity of its own, and the literary ride between the two covers of this anthology helps show that. What it all boils down to is . . . a thousand fish, swimming in a thousand mile circle of ocean, does not make a school of fish. They must first swim in a tight circle to become a school of fish. Bikerpoets are much the same.

The lone tree does not make a stand. A number of trees must group together to make a stand; each tree has its own roots, and each tree has had its own share of sunlight and rain. So it is with each Bikerpoet within these pages; they all have their own roots and their own share of Bikerpoetry history.

When did the fish become a school? Would a tree a mile from another tree still be a stand? So it is with Bikerpoetry history.

For decades, there has been Bikerpoetry of one sort or another—the 1950's song "Black Denim Trousers and Motorcycle Boots" is an excellent example of this. It has also been mentioned that Jerry Garcia rode a chopped Sportster and read poetry, and also ran with Neil Cassidy of Beat Generation fame. Arlo Guthrie wrote his famous "Motorcycle Song" in the 60's. There are also many other examples from that era. Martin Jack also tells us of Beats showing up to Beat literary events on British motorcycles. Perhaps Hunter

S. Thompson and Michael McClure fit this description? But most likely these were but a single swimming fish or two with no true thought of ever forming a true school or Bikerpoetry movement.

Who knows just what light or promise attracts fish to form a school, or what wind blows the seed of a tree to form a single stand. We know the stand of trees when we stand in its shadow. And so it is with Bikerpoetry history, for long may this Bikerpoetry anthology cast its literary shadow.

Over the Centuries, there have been many draws for writers and poets, be it, academia with its draw for those with a thirst for knowledge, or 15th century Paris with its draw for Francoise Villon and Guy Tabarie with their thirst for wine and adventure, or be it as 18th Century Grub Street London with its draw of Grub Street publishers with their promise of ink and sheckles.

For today's Literary Bikerpoetry Movement there have been many draws and definitive moments, some personal and some collective. Personal, such as my falling madly for the lore of the motorcycle at eight years old, or at sixteen my first solo ride down the black top or in 1965 my writing my first Biker prose piece. Or collectively, such as meeting up with Lizard Smith in 1976 and us discovering (as if bears need IDs to recognize one another) that we both rode and wrote. Or, singular and personal again, as in 1983 when I received my first paid ink for a Biker prose piece in a local newspaper.

If I hold any claim to fame, it is because I have always tried to hold my integrity as a Biker. I went to college, I worked on the college newspaper, and I published my own literary mag (*Wail! Magazine*). I produced a cable TV show and hosted numerous benefit shows, and almost every event photo will hold witness that I did all this as a leather-vested, motorcycle-boot-wearing Biker all along the way.

In the 1980's, I met Colorado T Sky in an auto-body shop. He and I did an almost immediate impromptu Bikerpoetry reading (literally within moments after our introduction to one another) for a group of Hippies sitting on oil cases and on paint buckets as the dust danced in the rays of the late afternoon sun.

In the late 80's, Sky and I started the Highway Poets Motor Cycle Club. The Highway Poets was Sky's name for the club, my first choice was The Roadpoets, which later became the name for my eMagazine—*Roadpoet eMagazine* (roadpoet.com). My dream and goal has always been to help publish others. During the 80's in my *Wail! Magazine* I published dozens of others, including Sky, and even today I always strive to publish others in whatever venue I find open to me.

Though Sky and I had started the Highway Poets, there were still not that many Bikerpoets in the club during those early days. We had a few Biker photographers, cartoonists, songwriters, and several dead-up journalists. Still, Bikerpoets at this point were in short supply. But I do remember Sky, early on, showing me Martin Jack's Bikerpoetry book. I had published my first Bikerpoetry chapbook (*Across an Urban Waste*) a year or two before this. Sky was to publish his first Bikerpoetry chapbook (*Sojourn*) shortly after this. Those days seemed so exciting then, much as the publishing of this anthology is now.

Throughout the 90's, there seemed only to be about a dozen or so Bikerpoets bumping around the country, banging out work here and there, and doing gigs. Today there seems to be dozens of Bikerpoets around the world and on the scene. One thing (I believe) that has helped increase the recognizable number of Bikerpoets in the public view is, like the long ago draw in Grub Street London, the draw of available publishers and ink, and today, a wide open Internet.

Today the Bikerpoetry community is blessed with many fine publishers, editors, and publications, such as our publisher here, Archer Books, Don Clady of the *Connecticut Cruise News Newspaper*, Jodi Lipson of motorcyclegoodies.com, Leo Castell of *The Motorcyclist's Post*, Q-ball of VTwinbiker.com, Gypsypashn's *Biker Bits*, my own roadpoet.com, Bear's roadpoet-ny.com, and MarySusan Williams Migneault's roadhousepress.com.

So, as we take full flight toward our Bikerpoetry future, we can know this anthology will stand as testament to the collective hard work and commitment to the Bikerpoetry movement by Bikerpoets themselves, and the publishers who have helped us along the way to make this happen.

In closing we hope you have enjoyed this Bikerpoetry anthology and that you will join us in looking forward toward future Bikerpoetry publishings, such as MarySusan Williams-Migneault's, *Bikerpoetry Comes of Age*, and my own *Bikerpoetry 101—The Early Years*, a collection of my Bikerpoetry 101 Columns from over the years.

—K. Peddlar Bridges, AKA The Peddlar

Contributors

Dr. Martin Jack Rosenblum
National Biker Poet Laureate, 2009 and 2010

Dr. Martin Jack Rosenblum is a lecturer in Music History and Literature at the University of Wisconsin-Milwaukee, Music Department, Peck School of the Arts; a recording artist on Rounder Records, and an artist endorsee for Gibson Guitars. Rosenblum is the recipient of an Academy of American Poets award for *Home* (1970), one of the numerous books of stark and evocative poetry he has written since the sixties. His autobiography was published in The Contemporary American Authors Series.

He is Historian Emeritus for the Harley-Davidson Motor Company, and on the Executive Board of Directors for the Les Paul Museum. His doctoral dissertation on the Objectivist Poets was the first, extensive scholastic investigation of this movement that is essential to a complete understanding of contemporary American poetry and still stands as a seminal, critical text. As a poet, Martin Jack is the author of the critically acclaimed book, *The Werewolf Sequence* (1974), that Allen Ginsberg proclaimed as being "mystical and practical."

As a singer/songwriter he is particularly known for the cult album, *Down on the Spirit Farm* (re-mastered in a *12ᵗʰ Anniversary Edition* in 2006), that (Little) Steven Van Zandt (of Bruce Springteen's E-Street band and *The Sopranos* HBO drama), called "Art Rock if there ever was any." Dr. Rosenblum's recent book, a significant history of American Vernacular Music and its aesthetic, is entitled *Searching For Rock And Roll* (2007). His latest album of original Rock songs with complex narrative lyrics is entitled *Ice Thorn: Singles Collection* (2007).

To bikers, his book, *The Holy Ranger: Harley-Davidson Poems* (1989), and the associated album, recorded with members of the Violent Femmes, *The Holy Ranger's Free Hand* (1990), stand for all that is Americana on a motorcycle or, rather, the modern cowboy's beloved horse as these works so depict the rider's outsider milieu. With the Holy Ranger project there was a new, alternative Americana movement defined through literature and music that pertained exclusively to biker poets and troubadours. Dr. Martin Jack Rosenblum's original poetry and rock and roll from this era, deeply rooted in American free verse and folk/blues idioms, received international critical acclaim, as does his recent work that continues to create visionary literary and musical idioms.

J.H. "Colorado T." Sky
National Biker Poet Laureate, 2007 and 2008

First published in 1969 and writing professionally since 1990, Sky's work has appeared in dozens of magazines, journals and anthologies in the US, Canada, Great Britain, Australia, South Africa and the former Soviet Union. He has received the MacMillan Prize for Poetry, Silver Spoke Prizes for Journalism and Fiction and has twice received the Eberhart Prize for Poetry. "First Light," the title poem of his second collection, was named Best Narrative at the 2001 Cambridge Poetry Awards. In 1992, Clay Douglas, editor of *Riders Xchange* magazine, dubbed him "the Poet-Laureate of the American Road." He is currently a staff writer for the *Harley Rendezvous Express* and publisher of the *Northern New England Review.*

A former U.S. Marine and lifelong biker, his hobbies include smoking too much, drinking too much and using too much salt. He doesn't belong to health clubs because he gets all the exercise he needs just pushing his luck.

He holds an A.A. from Cape Cod Community College (who named him Alumnus of the Year in 2005), a B.A. from Franklin Pierce College and an M.A. from Wright State University. He is currently pursuing his M. Ed. while investigating various Doctoral programs. National Secretary for the HPMCC, he is also a member of Phi Theta Kappa, Sigma Tau Delta, Psi Chi, The American Legion, The Association of Former Intelligence Officers, The Industrial Workers of the World, The Order of the Sword of Bunker Hill, The Veterans of Foreign Wars and the Whale Bay Police Motorcycle Drill Team. In his spare time, he is an Adult Literacy Instructor and Assistant Scoutmaster of Troop 586, Tipp City, Ohio.

Poet Biographies

DANIEL ABBOTT ARMSTRONG has been riding motorcycles since 1988, including a 1981 Suzuki GS450T, 1986 Ninja 600, 1993 Katana 750, and now rides a 2005 Triumph Speedmaster. The author of one chapbook and co-author of another, Armstrong has been writing poetry since grade school. After 35 years in SoCal, he moved to Frederick, Maryland, where he works as a computer support analyst and hosts a weekly poetry reading.

K. PEDDLAR BRIDGES is a Harvard graduate; co-founder of the HPMCC; First Biker Poet Laureate in New England; editor/co-founder of the original *Wail! Magazine*; and columnist for *Connecticut Cruise News*, *The Motorcyclist's Post* and motorcyclegoodies.com. He produced "Poets' Café," a cable television series, and has hosted poetry venues in Maine and Massachusetts. Peddlar rides a 2003 Harley-Davidson FX with a Roadpoet sticker on the windshield, and wears a Harvard patch on his vest. His license plate reads HD-POET.

MICHAEL R. BROWN is the author of four books of poetry, teaches high school English and directs plays in Down East Maine. His love of bikes arises from an afternoon spent in a bar in the Humboldt Forest with the Hell's Angels in 1972.

SUSAN BUCK has been riding motorcycles since 1986 and currently owns a 1970 BMW R75/5 and a 1994 H-D FXR. She served as editor of *Thunder Press East*, 1996-2000 and her words and photos have appeared in numerous motorcycle publications. Recipient of the Motorcycle Riders Foundation's Thomas Paine award for outstanding written advocacy, Susan Buck is noted for honest reflections as an experienced rider, while her photography combines journalistic and neo-psychedelic artistic styles, resulting in surreal, experiential truth. Susan joined the HPMCC in 2003 after several years of prospecting at the whims of Colorado T. Sky.

DON CLADY is the founder of Connecticut's Super Sunday (R) Expo and founder/publisher of the *Connecticut Cruise News* newspaper. His poem is dedicated to his late friend, legendary custom bike builder Indian Larry.

NEIL COTTER got his first biker experience at age eight. He has had just about every kind of motorcycle there is, and has ridden endless miles. After a bad accident, Neil spent three months in the hospital and another three years in rehab, coming to terms with the fact that his riding days are done. In the course of his rehab he found writing as a way of dealing with his emotions.

PAULA DOHERTY, a.k.a. "A Triumph Goddess," has been expressing personal experience through poetry for over 30 years. She's been riding and celebrating her own motorcycle for 19 years. Having owned six Harleys, Paula is now in love with her seventh bike, a 2006 Triumph Bonneville America.

DENIS J. DUNN is a US Veteran and a United Church of Christ minister in rural Maine. An avid biker, he's been published in various poetry journals including *Cafe Review*, *Passager* and others. Denis rides a Honda Goldwing, and has been riding Hondas since returning from Vietnam.

JOHN G. "ZONTAR" EDWARDS is the founder of The Poetry Club at Canada's largest high school, where he currently teaches. He has written policy for the Toronto District School Board and is an occasional columnist for the *Monitor* newspaper. He's also a drummer for Bullseye Records recording artists, Cheaper than Therapy. He rides a 1973 Ahmen Saviour chopper and a vintage BMW, and is a member of the HPMCC.

BLAZE ELLIOTT is a biker, poet, and artist. When she's not on the road working as a vendor at biker rallies and events, she rides an '84 Softail she calls "leper." Her work can be found in the *Connecticut Cruise News*, *RoadPoet* e-magazine, motorcyclegoodies.com and in hard copy in *Biker* magazine. And yes, blaze is really her name.

DICK EPSTEIN rides a '79 XS11 Yamaha. His first bike was a 150cc Honda he purchased in Vietnam in '69. He currently works as a technical writer in the Washington, DC area and still rides his bike every chance he gets. You can read more of Dick's poetry on his website, Memorialdaywritersproject.com

Poet Biographies

MARC D. "MOSHE" GOLDFINGER is currently the poetry editor of the Spare Change News, a Boston newspaper put out to benefit the homeless. He is a counselor for people with substance use disorders and some of his work has been used to augment courses at the University of Massachusetts in Boston. He is a member of the Highway Poets.

PANHEAD JOSH GRIFFITH hails from Cedar Falls, Iowa. He has a passion for restoring and custom building Harley-Davidson motorcycles and has been riding and writing for fifteen years. He rides a classic black and white 1954 FLE (Panhead) or his bobbed and flamed 1977 XLH (Ironhead). Panhead was the house poet for the ABATE of Iowa *Freeway Flyer* for six years. He's a prospective member of the Highway Poets and a staff writer for *RoadPoet* E-magazine.

BETH GROUNDWATER is SCUBA certified, learning tai chi, and has visited Machu Picchu, Angkor Wat, and the Galapagos Islands. Visit Beth's website at www.bethgroundwater.com.

THOM GUNN (1929-2004) was a British poet who emigrated to the United States in 1954. He settled in San Francisco and, over the course of his life, taught at Stanford University and the University of California at Berkeley, and published 11 books. His poetry often dealt with counterculture subjects, including motorcycles, drugs and AIDS.

DEBRA COPPINGER HILL is an award winning Cowboy Poet who has taught worldwide. Her biker poems reflect appreciation for the machines and lives of her closest friend and brother. "Cowboys of the trail . . . Bikers of the road . . . four legs or two wheels, it's all horse-power . . . freedom born into the blood." Visit her site: www.oldyellowslicker.com.

PRESTON HOOD's poems have appeared in *The Café Review, Michigan Quarterly Review*, Nimrod: *International Journal, Rattle, Salamander* and many other literary publications. Most recently, his book, *A Chill I Understand* (2006) won Honorable Mention in the 2007 Maine Literary Awards for published poetry.

Rubber Side Down

PATRICIA HOPE of Oak Ridge, TN, is a life-long biker, having owned a Harley, a Triumph and several Hondas. She's traveled across the Southeast and led many trips for The Touring Eagles. Her articles on these trips appear in *Rider*, Yamaha's *Venture Road* and several newspapers. She has written for the *Knoxville News-Sentinel* and *The Oak Ridger*, her hometown newspaper.

SUSIE HOWARD lives on Cape Cod, MA. Her work includes writing short stories, poems, book illustration, and using various media in the creation of visual art. In 1974 she pulled out of the Coliseum parking garage on 57th Street in NYC and headed west on an R90/6 Beemer. That bike was eventually replaced by a black 1000cc Beemer. She has ridden through Georgia, Alabama, Mississippi, Louisiana and Texas.

IBUNDA has been writing poetry since childhood. The "Sturgis 1969 trilogy" is part of her biker poems series. Her work has been published in several Dutch and Belgian magazines and poetry collections. She's been nominated for various poetry contests and has won the Festival of Freedom, which recalls the liberation of the Netherlands from WWII in May 1945. Samples of her work can be found on http://poeziefantasy.web-log.nl/.

BIKER JER is sixty years old and lives in West Virginia along the Ohio River. He's been riding Harleys since high school. Between bike rides, he drives an eighteen wheeler over the road. He has a website at www.bikerjer.com.

NIKOLAI IVANOVICH "NIKITA KARPUK" KARPUKOVICH, M.D., Ph.D. served his first assignment after medical school on a relief mission to Bangladesh in 1972. One of the first doctors on site after the Chernobyl disaster, he is recognized as one of the world's authorities on the treatment of radiation-induced illnesses. "Nikita" retired as a Colonel in 2004 after 32 years in the Russian Army, and now devotes his time to his three motorcycles (a Ural, a Zundapp and a CZ), his garden and his poetry. He has read and published throughout the former Soviet Union and the United States.

Poet Biographies

"CHOPPER" KATE JOHNSON lives, rides and writes from her home along the Mississippi River in Southeast Iowa. She rides a '95 Sportster and a '92 FLHS, both customized with the help of her husband. The bikes are her preferred modes of transportation. She's an associate columnist for *Roadhouse Press* and a member of the HPMCC.

MARY CAROL KENNEDY a.k.a. "Songbird" is a poet and musician. She is completing her Masters Degree in music in Cambridge, Mass. She resides in Maine and owns an '02 883 Sportster.

LINDA LERNER is author of twelve poetry collections. After a poetry reading in a cafe in Greenwich Village, she heard roars from rows and rows motorcycles ridden by metallic-leather clad bikers. Someone yelled out, "it's critical mass!" Thus the title of her poem. Her website is www.nyqpoets.net/poet/lindalerner.

BETSY (GYPSYPASHN) LISTER is from Massachusetss, where she is president of Lister Insurance Agency, Inc. She's also a biker columnist for *The Motorcyclist's Post*, motorcyclegoodies.com, and author of many articles on motorcycling and motorcycle insurance. Her Harley-Davidson motorcycles have been: 1996 XL883, 1996 Dyna Low Rider Convertible, 1997 Custom Road King, and she now rides a 2007 Street Glide. She was named Motorcycle Poet Laureate of New Hampshire 2005-2008, and of Massachusetts 2007-2008.

JACQUELINE M. LORING is an avid photographer and published poet. After receiving her Masters in Management from Cambridge College, she was named the executive director of the Cape Cod Writers' Center. She is a judge of the Veterans for Peace Poetry Contest and of poetry submissions for the *Cape Cod Times'* Prime Time Poetry Contest. She has written five scripts, two short plays and a full-length stage play that was read at the Provincetown Theater's Spring Play Festival.

IAN MACIAN is a former correspondent for the *Christchurch Star-Tribune*, an editor for Christchurch Press and a contributor to numerous journals, newspapers and magazines including

Australia's *OzBike*. He is the Highway Poets National Secretary for Australia and New Zealand. An ardent proponent of "literary journalism," he is a recipient of the Walkley Award and a Eureka Prize for Science Writing. Ian's been nominated for New Zealand's Prize in Modern Letters. His current rides include a 1975 Honda 750/4 and two BSAs: a 1941 WM 20 and a 1959 A-10.

CECIL "SPEEDO" PLAATJIES was a college student when he was arrested for insurgent acts against the apartheid regime in South Africa during the 1976 Soweto riots. Summarily convicted, he spent eight and a half years on Robben Island with Dennis Brutus and Nelson Mandela. Widowed while incarcerated, he was reunited with his daughter after his release. Today, they are both employed by the University of South Africa, she as a Lecturer in English and Afrikaans, and he as a custodian. His rides include a 1962 Vespa Van, a 1941 BSA and an AJS of dubious vintage. They still live in Soweto.

EDDIE "SOREZ THE SCRIBE" PLISKA has been writing biker poetry for well over 30 years. His earlier works have hit the pages of *EasyRiders* and *Outlaw Biker* magazines. His current ride is a custom chopped Triumph that he built. He is a Prospective Member of the HPMCC and currently writes for *Fastlane Biker* and *Behind Barz* motorcycle magazines, and is the House Poet for VTwin-Biker.com.

PREACHER has been riding since 1967 with "Grunt," his Shovelhead. He became a Christian, was called into the Ministry and attended Seminary 1993-97. He has a Bachelor of Arts in Biblical Studies with an English Lit minor, and an Associate of Divinity. He became the "Biker's Preacher" while in school, and after graduation began the mission of Planting Churches. Preacher has been writing poetry seriously since 1993.

"WILD BILL" ROGERS, in 1970 at age 15, moved to Alaska from Florida with his family. At thirty-five, he found his way into the saddle of a 1984 Harley-Davidson FXRP and, like so many before him, joined the pilgrimage to the Sturgis Rally in South

Dakota. Bill has also owned a 1990 1200 Sportster, a 1998 Dyna Wide Glide, a 1987 Kawasaki Vulcan 750, and his current ride, a 2004 Electra Glide Classic. He has maintained a website dedicated to biker poetry since 1994. "Wild Bill's Culture Corner" can be found at wildbill.tripod.com/biker.html.

TERRY ROZO divides her time between NYC and Provincetown, MA. She is currently working on her book, *Beyond Harlem: A Memoir*. Also a visual artist, Terry has shown both nationally and internationally. She is a recipient of an Art Matters grant, and The Louis Comfort Tiffany Foundation Award. Terry is one of the founding members of the women's motorcycle club, The New York Sirens. She rides a black, 2006, Honda CMX-250.

LAURENCE P SCERRI, a.k.a. Ironhorse Writer has spent over thirty years riding and writing. From Stingrays to Mini Bikes, Rice Rockets to Harleys, the roads of his life all led to one indisputable destination . . . to straddle a saddle. On the Web at www.ironhorsewriter.com.

LIZZARD SMITH is a southern-born biker, writer, musician and a retired member of the HPMCC. He now resides in Central New Hampshire. He writes what he calls Motoerotic poetry and Sonic Drama songs. Lizzard has owned, ridden and built Harleys, British bikes and large metrics. He has written stories, poems and essays, cut two records, and has been published in *The Motorcyclist's Post*, *The Saddle Bag Press*, *The Connecticut Cruise News* and on motorcyclegoodies.com. He is at present senior staff member for roadpoet.com.

TOM (WORDWULF) STERNERHOWE began to sing in the West Denver Housing Projects in the '60s. His passion is in the guttural growl of his Harley-Davidson. In 2003, SternerHowe edited the English translation of Hameed Al-Qaed's *Noise of Whisper*. He edited the Arabic to English translation of the poets of Bahrain, *Pearl, Dreams of Shell* which was published in 2007. He was nominated for the Pushcart Prize in 2006.

Wu "Woo Wu" Hai Tien is a former Chinese Bureau chief for the Japanese newspaper, *Far East*. He has also appeared in *The Straits Times* (Singapore), *Berita Harian* (Malay), the *Ming Pao Daily News*, *The Morning Post* (Hong Kong), *The Shipping Times* and *National Geographic*. In 2005, he was named "Storm King" by the Foreign Correspondents Association of Hong Kong for his award-winning coverage of the 2004 tsunami. A staunch opponent of government censorship, he is a former director of the Youth Press Association of China. His bikes include two Hondas and an antique Ming.

Roger Vagnarelli was born to an Italian father and Welsh mother in North Wales, UK. He lives in the southeast of England with his family, working as a mechanical design engineer. He performs both as a solo singer/guitarist and has a rock duo. He is an active member of the Harley-Davidson Riders Club of Great Britain and rides an H-D Dyna Superglide and Yamaha XT250. Writing poetry since his teens, his work has seen print, been heard on the radio, and both on the Web.

Diane Wakoski is the author of more than 20 collections of poetry, including *The Motorcycle Betrayal Poems* from Simon & Schuster in 1972 and *Emerald Ice* from Black Sparrow Press in 1989, reprinted by Godine in 2005, which won the William Carlos Williams prize from the Poetry Society of America. She has been Writer in Residence at Michigan State University since 1975. Currently, she is working on a new collection of poems, *The Diamond Dog*.

MarySusan Williams-Migneault has been editing and publishing biker poetry under the RoadHousePress imprint since 1986 (rdhousepress.com). MarySusan graduated Northern Essex Community College, then received her Bachelor of Arts Degree from Merrimack College in Massachusetts in 1990. She was a motorcyclists' companion for several years until a motorcycle accident ended her riding career. She has edited and written for the *Connecticut Cruise News*, motorcyclegoodies.com, *Bikerpoetry Comes of Age*, *Bikerpoetry 101* and *Bikerpoetry 202*.

Poet Biographies

J. Barrett (Bear) Wolf is editor of RoadPoet-NY.com, an online biker literary magazine. He rides a custom painted '97 Road King Police, and is a former decorated San Francisco Police Officer. He has taught motorcycle safety riding classes and is a member of the HPMCC.

Zwerver, The Dutch word for "Wanderer" is the road name of the poet Titus Waalwijk. He was born in The Hague, Holland. On his 16th birthday, Zwerver bought a chopped 50cc DKW police bike. In 1969, the year of *Easy Rider*, he started wandering in south England on his chopped 50cc, writing down what he saw. Now 53 and married, Zwerver still travels on the road to Germany, Belgium and France, and is a board member for the Holland motorclub, Easy Riders.

Special Contributor
Allen Ginsberg: Outside The Gearbox
Dr. Martin Jack Rosenblum

Allen Ginsberg proclaims everything to be holy in his poem, "Howl," for which he is culturally best known. William Carlos Williams, one of the fathers of American Free Verse, in his introductory essay to the City Lights book of the same title, takes special note regarding this young poet's energy for all things that others may overlook as being unfit for poetry. Even Williams himself would not take on these subjects—such as bikers. Allen raved about "crazy shepherds of rebellion" and when I first spoke with him in the early sixties this is precisely what he was looking for no matter where his search took him.

Ultimately, of all the Beat poets, it was Ginsberg who took the most risks culturally as well as artistically. "The bum's as holy as the seraphim" Ginsberg said, and so took kindly to motorcycle gangs such as Hell's Angels when the rest of the world ran away from them.

Without promoting violence of any kind and, in fact, to disrupt it, Ginsberg turned on the Angels and invited them into the next decade through Ken Kesey's Prankster revolution.

Ginsberg wrote esoteric postcards to me in the eighties about my own poetry and I recall thinking that outsiders are the essence of American Hip Culture and that the mainstream picks up on what's Hip and we get trends. I never got anything trendy from Allen. I only got what was holy. So did everyone, from bikers to rock musicians. Dylan got his credibility in "Subterranean Homesick Blues" from Ginsberg chants and the Angels got theirs from his celebratory holiness regarding who they were and, essentially, who they would become if they turned on, tuned in and dropped into the outer gear ratio.

Highway Poets
Motor Cycle Club
History

HPMCC Members, Laconia, NH, 2005
PHOTO BY HEATHER RUÉL
(l. to r.) J. Barrett (Bear) Wolf, Marc (Moshe) Goldfinger,
Colorado T. Sky, Susan Buck, José (JoeGo) Gouveia,
Betsy (GypsyPashn) Lister, and K. Peddlar Bridges

History of the HPMCC
Dr. Lukas Owdne

The inspiration for the Highway Poets Motor Cycle Club occurred on what was once a farm called Baldspot near Mullen, Colorado. One night, sometime in the fall of 1975, the usual suspects gathered around a campfire, which was pretty much the only social action available. There were four or five hippies, a couple of locals, an old backwoods dirt biker called Smokestack Lightning, and a younger biker poet, John "Nevermore" Raven. With them was a long-haired, red-haired, redneck poet (yup, named Red) who worked in a garage and came up on the weekends to hang out with his girlfriend and fix tractors. Red wrote raw but inspired love and nature poems in ballad meter. There was also this crotchety, manic-looking dude with tinted aviator shades who the bikers present later identified as gonzo journalist Hunter S. Thompson (somebody called him "Duke," somebody else called him "T"). And there was James T. Sky and Marie Amanda Bodé, the woman whom Sky remembers having the original idea to form a biker poets motorcycle club. Poetry and bikers? The hippies just had to hear this.

Everybody had been sitting around, all smoky and all, when one of the hippies (her name was Rainbow . . . or Starchild . . . or Oatbran) stood up and spontaneously, in a lovely, soothing voice, recited the "Desiderata," the soliloquy that starts "Go placidly among the noise and haste." The assembly was duly appreciative. Then Duke, donning those aviator shades, got up and rattled off "Jerkoff Jake, The Poolroom Snake, Who Fucked his Way North to

Duluth." In an instant, a poetry duel was on: Peace & Love versus Down & Dirty.

The hippies put up a good show. They trotted out Whitman, Dickinson, Frost, both Dylans, and some really good original stuff. Red did Marvel's "To His Coy Mistress," most of it, anyway, and pretty well. The bikers and manic Duke retaliated with some Dylan of their own, growling background dis-chords on "Highway 51," "It's Alright, Ma," and even took a stab at the "Subterranean Homesick Blues." These were followed with a volley of obscene odes and limericks: "Barnacle Bill the Sailor," "The Seven Crafts-men," and versions of "The Night Before Christmas" and "Kubla Khan" that most had never heard before.

The hippies were astounded. They didn't know that poetry like that existed. Once they stopped laughing, they christened these bik-ers, Smokestack, "Nevermore" Raven, Red, Duke and Sky, "The Dirty Birds."

A year later, "Nevermore" Raven vanished, but nowadays stills turns up in the occasional literary journal. Smokestack Lightning went back to the Rosebud Reservation and froze to death. He was found in his ancient Airstream the following spring. Marie Amanda died in a traffic accident. Sky left for northern California, where he met another one-eyed biker (also missing his right eye), also a poet, also named Sky. They eventually decided that he would be known as "California" Sky (because he'd been there right along) and our co-founder would be known as "Colorado" Sky (as he had recently arrived therefrom).

And so it went on, or didn't.

Sky returned from the left coast the summer of '77 and revived his membership in the MMA (the Modified Motorcycle Associa-tion) of Massachusetts. He was the Voice of the Wolfman at their fairly frequent '50s Nights, the music for which was provided out of Uncle T's (another local biker) extensive collection of mid-cen-tury 45s. Through '79, '80 and some of '81, Uncle T and Sky were neighbors in the same building out in the Lake region of Newton, MA. In nearby Boston, Sky got involved with the Stone Soup Po-ets and Jack "The Godfather" Powers. In a Massachusetts Avenue restaurant, Sky met K. Peddlar Bridges. Here, years after the idea had first surfaced were two biker poets. In '82 or '83, WMFO

Tufts radio broadcast (from the old firehouse out in Medford, MA) a reading by Allen Ginsberg and R. U. Outavit. After the event, Sky seized an opportunity to talk with Ginsberg.

Astounded by the concept that would become the HPMCC, Ginsberg replied, "The Highway Poets could be, for their generation, what the Beat Poets were for ours." Sky made up his mind to make it happen. Around that same time, Peddlar was at and around Salem State College, circulating among the literati there during his pre-Harvard days. He started *WAIL!* magazine and organized Roadhouse Productions. Throughout the 1980s, the orbits of Peddlar, Uncle T and Sky, as well as a few other prospects, suspects and hangers-on, started to close in around Boston and Cambridge, especially around the Stone Soup collective.

The organization was founded and officially named in 1990 in Cambridge, MA. Breaking stereotypes and crashing through cultural borders is never easy and often fatal. Still, the Highway Poets persevere; many combining their vocation and avocation in writing, publishing and, not surprisingly, teaching. As a profession that offers summers off, teaching is particularly attractive to biker poets, whose classrooms range from vocational education of at-risk youth to some of the world's most prestigious colleges and universities. Their message and methods have spread throughout the country and the world in the nearly two decades since initial conception.

Since 2002, the HPMCC has more than fulfilled the potential foreseen by Allen Ginsberg. New members joined from across the United States and around the world.

When Sky was a student at Franklin Pierce College, he had the honor of studying under Dennis Brutus of S. Africa, who shared a cell and split rocks with Nelson Mandela at Robben Island, for their involvement fighting apartheid. Through Brutus, Sky was able to connect with biker poets in the greater Johannesburg area. On the Internet he found the experiences of Russian biker poet Nikita, who rode his motorcycle through the Chernobyl area.

Peddlar and J. Barrett (Bear) Wolf started E-magazines, RoadPoet.com and RoadPoet-NY.com, respectively, while others did more online, allowing an ever-increasing number of biker poets to meet at the various intersections of the information superhighway.

Rubber Side Down

One rainy day in April 2003, the Highway Poets were reading at a coffeehouse in Derry, NH. they showed up in pick-up trucks; Peddlar said that although April is National Poetry Month, it rains too much for biker poets, and joked, "We need a summer month, like August, for Biker Poetry Month. With a serious look, Sky said, "Make it happen." Peddlar contacted editors of biker publications and organizers of bike rallies who endorsed the idea. 2008 marks the fourth year that the club will give twenty or more readings in August at Biker Poetry Month events.

The HPMCC currently has chapters, outposts and members in the United States, Canada, New Zealand, India, South Africa, Belarus, Japan and Singapore. The club seeks to establish chapters anywhere literacy and mobility intersect.

The Editor

José (JoeGo) Gouveia resides on Cape Cod, MA and has been published in 6 countries on 4 continents. Themes of his work include the polemic, family and gender, the erotic, the immigrant experience, the working class and the biker lifestyle.

About the Type

This book was set in Adobe Garamond™, a 1989 adaptation by Robert Slimbach of types cut by Claude Garamond (ca. 1480-1561) for the Parisian scholar/printer Robert Etienne in the first part of the 16th century.

After Garamond's death in 1561, the Garamond punches surfaced in the printing office of Christoph Plantin in Antwerp, where they were used for many years, and still exist in the Plantin-Moretus museum. Other Garamond punches went to the Frankfurt foundry of Egenolff-Berner, who issued a specimen in 1592 that became an important source of information about the Garamond types for later scholars and designers.

The Adobe Garamond™ roman weights are based on the true Garamond, and the italics on those of punchcutter Robert Granjon (1513-1589), who worked for Plantin.

Designed by John Taylor-Convery
Composed at JTC Imagineering, Santa Maria, CA